Tony Martin was born in Te Kuiti, New Zealand, in 1964 and has worked in Australia since the mid-1980s. He has written and performed comedy for radio (*Martin/Molloy*) and television (*The D-Generation, The Late Show*). He has produced three ARIA Award-winning albums with Mick Molloy, and his stand-up comedy was nominated for the Melbourne International Comedy Festival's Barry Award. He was the writer and director of the feature film *Bad Eggs*. And the voice of 'Bargearse'.

TONY MARTIN
Lolly Scramble
A memoir of little consequence

PAN
Pan Macmillan Australia

First published 2005 in Pan by Pan Macmillan Australia Pty Limited
1 Market Street, Sydney

Reprinted 2005 (twice), 2006, 2009, 2010

Copyright © Tony Martin 2005

The moral right of the author has been asserted.

All rights reserved. No part of this book may be reproduced or transmitted by any person or entity (including Google, Amazon or similar organisations), in any form or by any means, electronic or mechanical, including photocopying, recording, scanning or by any information storage and retrieval system, without prior permission in writing from the publisher.

National Library of Australia
cataloguing-in-publication data:

Martin, Tony,
Lolly scramble: a memoir of little consequence.

ISBN 978 0 330 42213 0.

1. Martin, Tony. 2. Television comedy writers – Australia – Biography.
3. Comedians – Australia – Biography.
I. Title.

791.45092

Typeset in 12/15 pt Bembo by Post Pre-Press Group
Printed in Australia by McPherson's Printing Group

Every endeavour has been made to contact copyright holders to obtain the necessary permission for use of copyright material in this book. Any person who may inadvertently have been overlooked should contact the publisher.

Papers used by Pan Macmillan Australia Pty Ltd are natural, recyclable products made from wood grown in sustainable forests. The manufacturing processes conform to the enviromental regulations of the country of origin.

For Annie

contents

Next Teller Please	1
Something of Dreams	17
Mono	36
Longnecks	53
The Secret Passage	71
A Made Bed in Hell	89
No Tarzan, Mind	114
The Yeti	137
Breakfast in Dubbo	164
Unlucky 12a	184
Prang	208
The Doctor is Out	222
The Notary Public	240
Any Old Iron	253
Donkey Shines	289
In the Eye of the Lolly Scramble	308

Names and particulars have been changed to protect the integrity of certain individuals and concerns, and, in one case, an already shaky marriage.

next teller please

I was standing in a room my grandmother insisted we call the 'scullery', attempting to hold the light switch exactly halfway between on and off. As any seven-year-old knows, this will produce a satisfying electric crackle and cause the light to flash joltingly, as if the house is being struck by lightning. I could do that for hours.

'Tony, stop doing that, you'll cause a fire.'

According to my mother, anything could cause a fire. Even brushing your teeth too vigorously or skidding on the lino.

'I'm bored.'

'All right then,' she said. 'Why don't you come with me to the bank?'

'Can I, Mum? *Can* I?'

Te Kuiti – a town I once heard described on

television as 'the jewel in the heart of New Zealand's King Country' – was, in the early seventies, the kind of place where going to the bank with your mum was as exciting as it got.

I had never once set foot inside a bank, but I had seen plenty of them on TV. From what I could tell, banks existed only to be robbed. I was yet to see a bank *not* being robbed. Why would there be a scene in a bank if it weren't being robbed?

Sadly, there was no robbery that afternoon, not even an elderly security guard asleep on his folding chair. But we did get to walk through the little rope maze and I was introduced to the manager, Mr Combover, as my mother later called him. He welcomed me to the exciting world of banking and gestured grandly towards a stand of pamphlets. While Mum made a withdrawal – in coins – I busied myself with the traditional business of filling out a deposit slip using only rude words, and hiding it three down in the pile, ready for discovery by, hopefully, an old lady.

My mother popped her coins into her purse, her purse into her clutch bag, her clutch bag into her handbag and her handbag into her shoulder bag. Our thrilling excursion over way too soon, we headed back to the Morris Minor. I was holding my complimentary plastic moneybox, in light blue for boys. It was moulded into the shape of a pig standing astride a treasure chest. What a strange view the bank had of itself. But, as I later discovered, a not inappropriate one.

'Listen up, class. This afternoon we will be welcoming a very special guest speaker,' announced Mrs Beauchamp with barely contained indifference.

As we were ten-year-olds and this was Thames South Primary, we knew this very special guest speaker would be either: the man in the white coat with the two glass boxes, one containing a healthy pink lung and, in the other, what appeared to be a dog turd; or, as was the case on this occasion, the man in the short-sleeved shirt from the Post Office Bank.

After distributing the complimentary plastic moneyboxes, by now gold and in the shape of a skyscraper, Mr Shortsleeves got down to the business of School Banking and Our Role In It. We were each issued a passbook account, which already contained the generous sum of ten cents. It was explained that the bank was our friend and that it would remain so for the rest of our lives. By depositing our money with the bank we would be securing our futures. And the more we deposited, the more secure this future would be. Look, here's a picture of a boat. And here's a picture of you. Now, how do we get you . ... onto the boat? By banking, of course.

Not only was the bank keen to get us all onto a boat, it had come up with a foolproof way to make this happen: competition. Each class would be pitted against the others in a weekly competition to see who could bank the most money with the Post Office. The winning class would, for that week, play host to the much-coveted school banking shield, a varnished wooden shield covered in smaller brass shields, each one engraved with the name of a class that had won the annual version of the competition. This competition was waged week after week, year after year, for the entire time I attended primary school, and like everyone else I gave so little of a shit about it, by the time I moved onto high school I had saved all of $28.85. When I went in to close my account, Mr Shortsleeves counted out the notes and coins, sealed them in an envelope and handed them to me with a fixed grin. The boat was never mentioned.

The trick with school banking was to deposit the absolute minimum amount that would still keep your class in the running for the shield. If your mum gave you ten cents, you would deposit five, or less, and pocket the difference. It was a sweet little arrangement and nobody rocked the boat. Occasionally, a new kid would play high-roller and flip a twenty cent coin on the desk when the monitor came round, but he or she was very quickly taken aside and set straight. The shield was always presented to the winning class at Friday assembly and, to the constant frustration of Mr Shortsleeves, the winning total was usually something like $1.79.

Every now and then a memo would be sent home to parents, complaining about the small amounts being banked, and we would have to up the deposits 'til the heat died down. Then it would be back to one and two cent pieces. One time I even tried to deposit a milk token.

But there was one thing about banking that did appeal to me – the passbook. The passbooks were only issued to their respective holders for the duration of the weekly banking session. The rest of the time they were locked away in the teacher's desk. We weren't allowed to take them home – this was the key to the money-siphoning scam – and so they were ours to fondle for only a few tantalising minutes every week. I came to treasure these brief moments alone with my passbook. I liked the way it looked, felt and smelt. I liked the way it fitted in my pocket like a passport, and as Mr Shortsleeves explained to us time and time again, it *was* a passport . . . to our futures.

But years later the bank would try to revoke these passports, and the 'friendship' would be sorely tested.

'You realise, Mr Martin, you're getting little-to-no interest on that passbook account.'

I'd been hearing that exact sentence with increasing frequency. It began as an occasional friendly reminder but had become, in the last six months, an insistent whine, which was clearly the shrill public whistle of a boiling corporate kettle. The passbooks had to go, and would you stragglers please get with the fucking program.

'You do realise that, don't you?'

I recited the usual lines. 'Yes, I know. I really like the passbook, that's all.'

'But there's little-to-no interest.'

'Yes, why *is* that? Why are you punishing me for my lifelong loyal support of the passbook system?'

'There're other accounts, with better interest. You get a card, you can use the ATM, there's Internet banking.'

'You just want me out of the bank, don't you?'

'I'm sorry?'

'That should be your catchphrase: "Get out of our bank!" I remember when it was "Come talk to us", now it's like "*Get the fuck out!*"'

It was usually about now that the teller called for someone else to come and explain it to me properly. Or ask me to leave. 'Fuck' never sounds good in a bank. I should have just smiled and said, 'Yes, I'm aware of that fact, ma'am, but I'm quite happy with my present financial arrangements, thank you very much,' and then I could have been on my way. But I could never do that. Mr Shortsleeves had explained to us that the bank was, and always would be, our friend. And I like to visit my friends in person, not talk to them on the Internet. Or through a slot in the side of their house. Especially when I'm giving that friend all my money to look after.

'Is there a problem here?'

'I was just explaining to Mr Martin that the passbook account gives him little-to-no interest.'

'You've heard about our new SuperSaver account, sir?'

'Yes. Many times.'

'No interest in that?'

'Little-to-none.'

'Most people are going over.'

'Is it compulsory?'

'No, it's your choice. It's simply —'

'I like the passbook.'

'Uh-huh.'

'I like the way it looks, smells and feels. It's like my passport.'

'Your what?'

'To the future.'

They just looked at me. 'Are you unwell?'

And that's pretty much a conversation I've had every week for the past several years. They don't want to get rid of the passbook *completely* because even they – in their appalling corporation couture – are aware that there is a certain amount of style and tradition associated with the passbook. There's that cardboard it's made from, and the chattering machine the teller feeds it to, the one with the occasional overbite.

'I'm sorry, Mr Martin, it seems to have printed

over the top of the previous entry, so I'll write the balance in for you.'

A handwritten balance in a passbook. Can you imagine such a thing? They know that the passbook is the last vestige of actual character in their soulless downsized shopfront. So long as they hang onto the passbook, they're like a cinema that still has a cat.

'Oh, and you realise you're getting little-to . . .'

'*Yes*. Yes, I do.'

Leave it, Tony. For god's sake, leave it at that.

'Oh . . . all right. I'm sorry. Only doing my job, that's all.'

'Your job? You won't *have* one if you talk everyone into *Internet fuckin' banking!*'

Asked to leave.

For a long time I wondered why it was that I always seemed to lose it in the bank. Having them go on about the little-to-no interest every time I made a transaction had a lot to do with it. But what about those queues? I think the bank likes to keep the queues long to convince people to choose Internet banking or the ATM, and *get the fuck out so we can start sacking people.*

For a few months I had a sure-fire way of dealing with bank-queue frustration. If I found myself standing in one for longer than twelve minutes — the time, I had observed, when someone usually snapped — I would walk to the front of the line, turn to face the exasperated crowd, and recite the following: 'Everyone, let's have a big round of applause for the shareholders, whose relentless series of branch closures has provided us with the endless wait we're enjoying here this afternoon.'

And without fail, after a couple of dumbfounded seconds, the queue would break out into a genuine round of applause, just long enough for me to make it to the nearest exit. It was a great feeling, but in fairness, not everyone clapped. There would always be one person executing the international semaphore for male self-abuse. (I note that when rendering this pantomime, the performer always accords himself a member of equine proportions.)

Of course, I could never visit that particular branch again, but this was in the days when that was still an option. I was always careful to 'keep myself nice' with the bank nearest my house.

But the fourth time I performed this routine, here's what happened. I walked to the front of the line, turned to face the exasperated crowd, and recited the following: 'Everyone, let's have . . .'

And at that exact moment the alarm went off, and *ker-blang ker-blang*, up came the metal screens. Because the branch was too small to have its own security guard, there followed several awkward seconds where nobody did anything. The only sound was the steady shriek of the alarm. What exactly was supposed to happen next? The staff were presumably cowering behind the sheet of metal; were the cops on the way? My audience seemed 'pissed off' rather than the 'laudatory' my ego demanded, so I decided to walk calmly towards the door, my head held high in a misguided attempt to retain some shred of dignity. As I approached the end of the queue, a solitary little old lady made a brave attempt to get a round of applause going. No-one joined her.

I walked home with my collar up, pathetically trying to look like, say, Mickey Rourke back in the days when he looked like Mickey Rourke. I made a mental note to cross that branch off my list. There was no need. It closed two-and-a-half weeks later.

Soon after this, I began to notice that the tellers were starting to back off. The little-to-no interest went unmentioned for weeks at a time. What had happened? Had word gotten round? Surely not, as I had seen many, many others go mental at the bank, using language and gestures far more florid, far more obscene than my own. Admittedly, I'd not seen anyone else trigger the metal screens, but as I'd never been formally pinged for that, in the end, harmless piece of tomfoolery, that couldn't be the reason. Could it be that I, and others of my ilk, were finally starting to win this decade-long war of attrition?

Then one day I observed something new. Something fleeting but perhaps significant. The teller had completed the transaction and was just about to return my book. I could feel a 'You realise . . .'

coming on when, almost as an afterthought, she glanced at her computer screen, paused, and then simply handed back the book, saying nothing.

What was that? Was it even anything?

I dismissed it.

Then it happened again. And again. Was it my imagination, or was there something written about me on the screen, an editorial note on my file or page, or whatever? I had to know. The next time it happened, I confronted the issue head-on.

'Excuse me, is there some problem with my account?'

'No, I don't think so. Why do you —?'

'Well, I noticed the way you . . . *reacted* when you looked at the screen just then. Is there something I should know about?'

'Not at all, Mr Martin. It's nothing.'

What could I do? I couldn't demand to see the screen, like some conspiracy theory nutbag.

'Can I help you with anything else?'

'No. That's it.'

'Thank you for banking with us.'

But it was driving me crazy. Was there something on my file? Had I been labelled a troublemaker, a difficult customer, a hothead prone to explosive outbursts when provoked? Was I on some kind of blacklist?

How had the 'friendship' descended to this level of mutual mistrust?

I never did find out. One time, when the teller was off sorting out some traveller's cheques, I toyed with the idea of reaching across and turning the screen around. Of finding the line that read, 'Easily enraged by requests to relinquish passbook' and changing it to 'Possessed of a ten inch penis'. But the memory of the guillotine-like screens put paid to that.

'Thank you for banking with us.' I can still recall the first time I heard a teller come out with that bizarre stilted benediction. Now it is part of the ritual. We understand that the social transaction has not been concluded until those six market-tested words have been intoned with robotic sincerity. But the first time, I had no idea it was coming.

'Thank you for banking with us.'
'Sorry?'
'Um . . . thank you. For banking with us.'
'Sure, I —'
'Bye-bye.'
'I didn't realise you . . . is this something you've been wanting to say . . .?'
'It's just a general thank you. Don't worry about it.'
'Okay, sorry. But . . . you sounded so . . .' I wanted to say *desperate*.
'Please, don't worry about it.'
'Is everything *all right* here, at the bank?'
'We're fine. Everything's fine. It's a new thing they've introduced.'

'Gratitude?'

'Just forget it. Forget I ever said it.'

But friends don't forget things like that. The bank was clearly reaching out. 'Thank you for banking with us,' it had blurted. I read it as a cry for help.

Two Christmases later, I had to fly to Perth to honour a longstanding commitment. I was met at the airport by a man called Porkstorm. 'Name's Porkstorm,' he announced. 'Lost all the weight, but the name was so good, I've hung onto it.'

Porkstorm was wearing a T-shirt emblazoned with a flaming marijuana leaf, which was partly obscured by a laminated pass from the Melbourne Grand Prix that, he informed me, he'd kept around his neck since the event itself, six weeks earlier. He hadn't taken it off once, not even while, as he put it, 'on the job'.

He led me to his vehicle, which was far from Grand Prix standard. It was what you might call a 'shaggin' wagon' or, if you were my cousin Shane, a 'fuck truck'.

'Move any of that shit out of the way, mate,' he said, quickly drawing the curtain that partitioned the cabin from the velvet-lined paradise in the back. The passenger seat was piled high with smoking paraphernalia and porno mags. This bloke was ready for anything.

'Rollie?'

'Not for me.'

Porkstorm was one of those drivers who could negotiate all the twists and turns of an airport carpark while rolling a perfect cigarette on his lap.

'Who's your team, mate?'

'I, uh . . . I don't have one.'

'What? You're from Melbourne, aren't you?'

'Well, yes, but I don't know anything about football.'

'Right. Okay. Fair enough.'

I could feel myself dropping several notches in Porkstorm's estimation.

'You follow the cricket?'

''Fraid not.'

A long exhale of disbelief filled the cab with smoke. And that is where the dialogue may well have ended, had I not spotted something peeking from the pocket of his boardshorts.

'Sorry, is that what I think it is?'

'What? Me bankbook?'

'You still have one of those?'

'Fuckin' oath.'

'You realise you're getting —'

'Little-to-no interest? Sick of hearin' that.'

Neither of us spoke. We just looked at each other, two slack-jawed grins sharing a moment. Then the lights changed and he was off. For block after block Porkstorm waxed lyrical on the manifold joys of the passbook. How you could simply flip it open and see how much money you had. How not having to post out monthly statements saved the ungrateful bastards approximately ten dollars per passbook-holder per year. How the little-to-no interest sorted the aficionados from the pretenders, and weeded out the passbook poseurs. It was everything I'd been saying for years.

The Perth scenery went begging as we inventoried the many tiny traditions that would die with the passing of the passbook. The complimentary little plastic sleeves, kept in a drawer. The invisible signature revealed only by the glow of the magic purple light. The grim ritual of stamping every single page with an irreversible 'Cancelled' once the book was full.

I told Porkstorm of my many heated encounters with passbook-dissing tellers 'just doing their job', and he revealed that he too had occasionally been asked to leave the premises merely for presenting a spirited defence of a system that was, after all, 'their fuckin' idea in the first place'. He claimed to know of other staunch passbook-holders, 'compatriots', he called them, and he told me of one bloke who had every single one of his passbooks, going right back to childhood, mounted on a special shelf in his study. Why hadn't I thought to do that? If only I'd kept them. Imagine that.

High on a torrent of passbook lore, I agreed to join my fellow traveller for 'a couple of quieties' at a beer garden in Fremantle he claimed came with the imprimatur of one Bill Hunter. It was an invitation too good to refuse.

We parked ourselves in a corner and Porkstorm spent a good forty-five minutes speaking of his life in Freo. Something about a decent-paying job, a friendly ex-wife, some shit-stirring kids and a bevy of colourful mates, one of whom could get 'flash stuff cheap'. It was the enviable testimony of a man who had it all, and had it all wholesale. I remember none of the details. I was focussed only on what he was using for a coaster beneath his tall, gleaming glass of beer.

something of dreams

Colin Plympton was one of the fattest kids at Thames South Primary and I was possibly the thinnest. This made it difficult for us to be seen together, either in the playground or on the way to and from school. The visual juxtaposition was so amusing that no-one could let it pass without comment. And if we ever sat next to each other in class, by the end of the period at least three new 'Fatty and Skinny' couplets would be circling the room, each one filthier than the one before.

Fatty and Skinny,
Sitting in class . . .

Whatever came next, you can be sure 'class' would have been rhymed with 'arse', and that the verse would end with me crushed beneath it. The arse, that is.

If Colin and I wanted to speak during school hours, an intermediary would have to be employed, and if we wanted to talk in person, we would have to meet at his home or mine, alone or in the company of equally silhouette-challenged sympathisers. It was like we were undercover cops forced to meet at a series of designated safe houses. My place was preferable, as Colin's dad was himself the creator of some of the most graphic Fatty and Skinny rhymes, despite being the unmistakable genetic source of Colin's formidable girth and many competing chins.

Most eleven-year-olds, if backed into this corner, would probably seek out more conventionally shaped friends, but Colin and I shared identical interests: TV, movies, comics and smashing things. And identical dislikes: the pool and the beach. Neither of us was able to appear in public wearing swimming costumes without attracting unfavourable comparisons to, respectively, whales and sticks. As Thames was, if nothing else, a seaside community, Colin and I often found ourselves loitering together in long pants, while the beautiful people cavorted nearby in their lollybags. We were like two John Merricks appearing on *Baywatch*, and through this a partnership was formed.

One weekday afternoon during the school holidays, Colin and I were sitting in his bedroom trying to work out why none of the Terence Hill–Bud Spencer movies were listed in the *Halliwell's* film guide that we tag-team loaned in two-week blocks from the public library. This fortnight it was at Colin's place, so that was where we'd headed after the matinee screening of *Watch Out, We're Mad*, a movie we had both deemed 'a masterpiece'. We had thought *Trinity Is Still My Name* unsurpassable, but this one had dune-buggies!

I had just discovered that Terence Hill's real name was Mario Girotti and that someone else did his voice, when Colin called me to the window.

'Someone's parking across Frank Tugald's driveway. He'll go spastic when he sees that. Let's go and get a good seat.'

'Wait! Look at this lot.'

Colin's bedroom was on the first floor and we watched agog as the station wagon popped its doors and expelled what looked like a swarm of hippies, clutching clipboards and cardboard tubes. This was already the most interesting thing that had happened in weeks.

'Who are they? What are they looking at?'

Two of the hippies were holding their tubes up to their eyes and scanning the street, while the others pointed and scribbled notes. It was like a piece of impromptu street theatre. Mrs Plympton would freak when she saw them.

'One of them's coming in here!'

'Come on, we can't miss this.'

The *Halliwell's* was tossed aside as we ran for the stairs like 'a herd of stampeding elephant,' as Mrs Plympton liked to say. 'I might as well bring in Whelan the Wrecker,' she'd sigh, making use of an expression she'd successfully imported from Australia.

When we got to the front door, she was already in conversation with a young woman whose skirt she would later describe as 'leaving little to be discovered on her wedding night'.

'You want to *what*?'

'We'd like to use this street in the background of a TV show. Your house would be in shot and because it's set forty years ago, we're asking everyone if they wouldn't mind taking down their TV aerials. It'd just be for one afternoon.'

Colin and I could not believe what we were hearing. A TV show? What TV show? As far as we knew, TV shows were made overseas. Sure, there were one or two rather tatty local productions, but they weren't real TV shows like *The Six Million Dollar Man* or *The Bionic Woman*. There were no bionic New Zealanders on our screens at all, just a man in a dinner suit reminding us to 'Stay tuned for *Country Calendar*'.

'Well, I don't know about this. My husband won't be home 'til tonight. I don't know that he'll want our house appearing on the goggle-box.'

'Muuuuuuuummmmm!' The whine went up like an air-raid siren, and despite Mrs Plympton not being my mother, I jumped on board halfway, providing Colin with a perfectly pitched backing vocal.

'Colin, I'm talking with this young lady here. Where are your manners?'

'Mumwehavetoletthemuseourhouseonthetelly! Wehaveto!'

'I'm not sure your father would . . .'

'CallDadatwork! CallDadatwork!'

Colin was gripping the front of his mother's lemon slack-suit so tightly, I thought he might be about to tear it clean off. Mrs Plympton turned back to the girl from the goggle-box. 'It's not a permissive program, is it? With nudity or swearing?'

'No, not at all. It's for children. It's historical.'

'With educational content?'

'Most definitely.'

'A moral viewpoint?'

'Yup.'

'Tastefully presented?'

'Of course.'

Having established that the show would be shithouse, Mrs Plympton agreed to canvass the matter with her husband that night. Colin and I looked at each other and each knew immediately what the other was thinking: the house would be in shot, therefore the windows would be in shot, and therefore anyone standing in one of those windows would be . . . ON THE TELLY! Like Steve Austin, 'a man barely alive'.

The game was afoot.

Mr Plympton quite liked the idea of his house featuring in the background of a show we knew only as *Something of Dreams*. It may have been *Kingdom* or *Quest* or even *Street of Dreams*, but within a week we had all decided it was *Something of Dreams*, and henceforth that's what we would call it. Mr Plympton's newly erected front fence was, in his eyes, a veritable 'Fence of Dreams' and he seized the opportunity to parade it before a national viewing audience.

'Wait 'til your Uncle Leo in Invercargill clocks a look at it!' he told Colin. 'That pagoda of his never made it into that plane crash show they shot down there.'

Now everyone had a vested interest in *Something of Dreams*. Even Colin's mum was having the curtains redone. Up and down the street we would hear about someone who was painting their roof or remodelling their front garden or, in one case, installing a fountain. The street had been chosen because, aside from the TV aerials and the odd large wooden butterfly, the houses all looked pretty much as they would have in the 1930s. The street curved down a hill, meaning a wide shot from the bottom would reveal at least twenty of them, so all these sudden renovations had to be kept 'in period'. Mrs Nagle at number 24, always keen to stay one step ahead of her neighbours, invested in a second-hand penny farthing bicycle, which she kept tethered next to her front door. It didn't look very 1930s to me and neither did the fully operational stocks that materialised in front of Frank Tugald's place, a sombre warning to anyone who dared park across his driveway. It was madness. The shoot was six weeks away and already Colin's street was turning into a pissweak colonial theme park. I was pretty sure the TV people would make everyone change it all back. They'd have to dirty up the new paint jobs and roll away the enormous number of wagon wheels that had started appearing on people's front lawns.

The day of the shoot was known to all as 'Aerial Day', as that was the day the men of the street would ascend their own houses, in unison (Colin's dad wanted to get some Super-8 footage), to remove the troublesome TV aerials. I pictured them as a line of dancing chimney sweeps, outlined against the sunrise, launching into a jaunty cockney musical number. Perhaps that too would be on the telly – in the 'making-of'. Who knew what glorious delights lay ahead? We were in show business. Actually, I myself lived seven blocks over, but on the day I would be there, standing very still in Colin's bedroom window, dressed as the young Abraham Lincoln.

But the *Something of Dreams* affair, to which we will return in a moment, was not my first pre-*E! News* glimpse behind the skirts of showbiz. Several years earlier my then school, Te Kuiti Primary, had played host to a visiting celebrity. Frankly, at age seven, in that obscure town in the King Country, you could have shown me a rock that had appeared in an episode of *Boney* and I would have gone all starstruck and weak at the knees. But this was no rock, it was 'Skippy the Bush Kangaroo' herself. The real one, flown first-class across the Tasman, to be trotted out at every primary school fete and gala day, where twenty-five cents guaranteed you a handshake and a paw-smudged 'autograph'. The line went around the block. It was, as the *Chronicle* put it, 'Kangamonium!'.

I had always suspected that on the TV show, Skippy's paws, when shown in close-up, were not her real paws. Even at seven, and having never seen a real kangaroo, I felt there was something too dexterous about the way Skippy seemed to point at things, draw lines in the dirt, grasp objects and, in one episode, crack a safe. Now I would be able to confirm my suspicions up close. Carefully, I unwrapped the coins from the twist of newspaper my mother had slipped into my top pocket, paid the fee and received my 8 × 10 glossy of the star, posed winsomely before that helicopter. I took my place in the queue and twenty minutes later, there I was, three kids away from being face-to-face with someone I'd only ever seen on the telly. A star. One with a dirty secret I was set to expose. At last we would see just what those magic paws could do away from the cameras. In my pocket was a ballpoint and my plan was to challenge the nimble-fingered marsupial's handler to let the creature try to pick it up. But, as I should have realised by then, no-one ever gets one over on that feisty roo.

'Get back! All of you, get back!' A ruckus was unfolding at the front of the queue. 'I told you, no sudden movements!'

Skippy, it appeared, was going apeshit. A five-year old had apparently tried to hug the kangaroo as she executed an autograph with, it has to be said, considerable human assistance. The roo had suddenly snapped and was now kicking and flailing on the end of her leash. As screaming children and parents scattered, one of the handlers barked into a walkie-talkie and dragged the thrashing animal back behind the spangly curtain. Amidst a burst of feedback, the not-properly-cued *Skippy* theme exploded from the speakers and a man in mirrored sunglasses advised the crowd that the show was most definitely over.

As I wandered back to the car in a daze, still clutching my 8 × 10, that familiar chorus of child sopranos echoed around the playground, puncturing the waning melee with its irresistible sunny cheer.

Skippy, Skippy, Skippy, the Bush Kangaroo,
Skippy, Skippy, Skippy, a friend ever true.

There were no serious injuries.

★

LOLLY SCRAMBLE

My second brush with celebrity came when I found myself in the Hamilton studio audience of the annual TVNZ telethon. The telethon was a massively successful twenty-four-hour live fundraiser, famous for its incessant conga lines of minor-league celebrities singing 'Thank you very much for your kind donations!' over and over, until you had no choice but to phone in and pledge ten bucks, just to get them to shut the fuck up. Hamilton, being the fourth-largest but fifth most prestigious city in New Zealand, was well down the roster in the telethon celebrity draft, and subsequently got the names who weren't big enough for Dunedin. Dunedin got Mrs Marsh, the barrel-girl from *It's In The Bag!* and the man who did the nightly 'closedown' voice-over, so our hopes were never too high. A friend from school's dad had obtained tickets for a two-hour block on Saturday morning, and as I took my seat on the bleachers in the converted L.J. Ballroom, I speculated as to who might fill the three guest spots on the panel. I think Auckland had someone from *The Mod Squad* that year, possibly that bloke who'd said 'shit' on live TV in Australia the year before. No doubt TVNZ were hoping he'd do it again, this time for charity.

As the floor manager waved us into silence in preparation for our link-up with the national viewing audience, a man whose wide polyester lapels appeared to be chomping at his neck like a great white, jogged through a storm of applause and took his customary position at the head of the panel. It was newsreader Tom Bradley, an old pro who, with his smart casual demeanour, could conduct a grave interview with an afflicted child before being dunked in a tank full of green slime. Anything to get the national tally ticking over, thus triggering yet another conga line.

'Ladies and gentlemen, I'd like you to welcome our celebrity panel for the next two hours, the folks who are going to get the phones ringing and keep the laughs coming . . .'

We had lucked into an uncharacteristically high-wattage trio for 11am on a Saturday. Weightlifter Precious McKenzie received a thunderous welcome and pledged to spend the next two hours lifting things for muscular dystrophy. Next up was a woman who played the nosey neighbour on the TV soap *Close to Home*. Several people booed. They were shooshed. An argument broke out. Tom Bradley quickly distracted everyone by leaping onto the desk and performing twenty press-ups. The phones went mental. The conga music was cued.

Then, to audible gasps of awe, the third panellist was introduced. 'All the way from Hollywood, USA, from TV's *Alias Smith and Jones*, please welcome Ben Murphy!'

The crowd went nuts. It was 'Kid Curry' himself, who along with his partner 'Hannibal Heyes' robbed dozens of banks and trains but, as the opening narration reminded us, 'They never shot anyone.' Everyone in that Hamilton crowd was aware of the tragic irony that Pete Duel, the actor who played Hannibal Heyes, did in fact shoot someone, namely himself, and that he'd been replaced in the second series by the actor who did the narration – the guy who said the line, 'They never shot anyone.' But with Ben Murphy actually standing there before us, that suddenly wasn't so funny, and the applause lasted a full minute. Only Tom Bradley hitting himself in the face with a pie brought it to an end.

It was a few years after *Alias Smith and Jones* and Murphy was now known as the 'Gemini Man', a secret agent who could make himself invisible for one minute by using his digital watch to trigger special effects left over from the previous year's *The Invisible Man* with David McCallum. During an ad break the telethon crew set up a large blue screen behind Murphy and an elaborate sketch was prepared. It was explained that we were to watch the monitors and that Ben Murphy would demonstrate the incredible powers of the Gemini Man's digital watch.

'Three . . . Two . . . (nothing) . . . And we're back. And Ben, Mrs Del Fresnell of Dargaville says she'll donate fifteen dollars if you can make yourself invisible, like you do on your hit show *Gemini Man*, 8:30 Wednesdays on One.'

On that cue, Ben Murphy rolled up his sleeve,

flashed the startlingly modern watch and squeezed a button.

On the monitors he remained all too visible, while instead the background turned into a weather map. Murphy was unaware of this, of course, and began doing some 'invisible' acting. It was a debacle. But it was local content. After considerable confusion, the camera panned off 'The Gemini Weatherman', just in time to catch Tom Bradley tipping a can of purple paint over his head. For charity.

There were no big names in *Something of Dreams*. From what we could glean from the papers, it was one of those shows where some mischievous orphaned ragamuffins, their faces artfully smudged with charcoal, team up with a raffish, down-on-his-luck, urchin-friendly con man during the wacky days of the Great Depression. Cardboard speak-easies, too-shiny vintage cars, riddley-diddley banjo music and screwy racetrack scams galore.

'Blinkin' Jesus, you rascally tykes'll be the death of me, you mark my bleedin' words, gorblimey.'

'Give it a rest, Guv'nor! Wivvout our help you'd've never've rolled ol' Ernie Dingbat for them thirty nicker!'

'Fiddlesticks and flummery! You pint-sized scally-wags couldn't run a scheme or swindle on your ownsome todd. It's incon-blinkin'-ceivable. Now, where's me two-bob watch?'

'You mean *this* watch, Guv'nor?'

'Why I . . .'

Much laughter.

Freeze.

Roll credits.

Portions of this programme were shot outside the Plymptons' in Thames. Didn't that fence look nice? And the new curtains really helped. The Young Abraham Lincoln will return in *Something of Dreams 2*.

At least that's how I saw it playing out in my head. Colin was going one better. The TV people had warned that no residents would be allowed to appear as extras, as the story required that the street be deserted. But Colin was going to ask if he could be a dead body; say, a typhoid victim. A very well-fed typhoid victim. It was a foolish plan and I told him so.

'Typhoid? Why would there be typhoid? Isn't it a light-hearted caper like *The Apple Dumpling Gang*?'

'You saw *The Apple Dumpling Gang*?'

We both felt there hadn't been a good Don Knotts vehicle since *The Love God?*. We held strong views about film, and had already storyboarded our own short feature, which we hoped to shoot using Mr Plympton's Super-8 Chinon when we were old enough to be trusted with it. It was a proposed third 'Trinity' movie, called *For the Last Time, It's Trinity*, and would feature a series of spectacular fistfights, shot in and around the many abandoned goldmines that dotted the hills behind Thames. I would be Terence Hill and Colin, obviously, would be Bud Spencer. We had rehearsed the fight moves, the pile-drivers and the windmills many, many times, all from memory, as this was a few years before the VCR. *Something of Dreams* would be our first chance to see a real film crew in action and possibly steal some of their ideas. And if we could somehow wangle our way into shot, it would technically count as a screen credit and give us some much-needed credibility in the industry. Or, at least, the playground.

But then it all started to go horribly wrong.

Percy Quayle was a cranky old bastard in a shell-like cardigan who lived three doors up from the Plymptons. He'd been away when the TV crew had made their initial pitch to the residents, so his neighbour, Mrs Haupt, had vouched for him. When Quayle found out, he cracked the shits and announced that he wanted no part of this 'poofter endeavour', and that the 'mob from the telly can blow it out their arse, and mine'. Why they would need to blow it out his as well, he never bothered to explain.

It quickly transpired that there was no way Percy could stop the crew filming his house in a long shot, but he made it known that there was 'No fuckin' way I'm taking down me fuckin' aerial, so back up to that and take it for a spin.' Quayle's mystifying obscenities were always gleefully related to us by Colin's dad, once he was certain his wife was out of earshot. Mr Plympton was acting as a go-between for the TV people and the disgruntled Quayle, and always came home with an earful of nonsensical abuse.

'Then he tells me why should he go out of his way to help the TV mob when they're the ones showing all the bloody ads, like that has some relevance. I'm telling you, lads, that man is four-alarm bloody fruitcake.'

That evening we ate in silence. Was this obstinate crustacean about to spoil it for everyone? Surely the TV people would simply find another street, one where the residents were a bit more cooperative and comprehensible?

'Couldn't they just frame his roof out, Dad?'

'Frame his roof out? Very good, Colin. You're still not getting that camera.'

'Couldn't they just tilt down and crop out his aerial?'

'He's right smack-bang in the middle of their shot. It's a no-win.'

The next morning Mr Plympton made one final entreaty to the grumpy old coot and came back shaking his head.

'What did he say? What did he say?'

'Something about how, ever since he refused to take part in this circus, his TV reception has gotten steadily worse. And something else about taking a dump out the front of his house on the day of the filming, and let them put that on the TV.'

'It couldn't hurt,' I said, making the most of a rather obvious opportunity. 'They ran *Apple's Way*.'

No-one laughed. Then I remembered that the Plymptons liked *Apple's Way*. I should have said *The Waltons*.

'I'll just have to call the TV people,' said Colin's dad, as though this were the sort of thing he said every day.

He disappeared into his study to make the call, and we saw our dream disappearing with him. We would no longer be featured extras in a major new television event. We would simply be Fatty and Skinny, sitting in a tree, waiting for the arse joke in line number three.

The Plymptons' street appeared in *Something of Dreams* for all of seven-and-a-half seconds. It was a single wide shot and as soon as it began, an actor we had never heard of walked into frame, completely obscuring Mr Plympton's new fence. After looking up and down the street, he frowned, exited frame and they cut to a shot of a vintage car wheel slicing through a mud puddle, accompanied by banjo music. There was no subliminal appearance by the young Abe Lincoln, nor were any bloated typhoid victims seen rolling into view. The TV people had people to make sure that sort of thing didn't happen, and so we were all herded into a roped-off area, well behind the camera. A battered trestle table, a steaming urn and a single plate of Arrowroot biscuits stood as an accurate reminder of the state of the New Zealand film industry. And I noticed that the actor, rather than stepping into an enormous trailer, simply popped behind a car and changed into his dusty 1930s suit right there on the footpath.

'You can't see the fence,' said Colin's dad.

'You can't see the curtains,' said Colin's mum.

'You can't see us,' said Colin.

'I can still see that penny farthing,' I said, moments before it was hauled away.

'When's old Percy coming out to take that dump?' wondered Colin, to the amusement of all but his mother.

'He's just over there,' said Mr Plympton, and he was. Even Percy Quayle, the most vocal opponent of the entire 'homosexual farrago', was standing in the roped-off area, lured by the irresistible glamour of filmmaking and the biscuits. He was chewing on an Arrowroot and staring intently at something just in front of the camera. Percy had remained steadfast in his refusal to take down his aerial, but it seemed the TV mob had thwarted him again. The camera was bolted to a tripod, and positioned between the lens and the vista before it was a sheet of glass standing on an easel. A man resembling Catweazle was carefully painting a small section of sky directly onto the glass, thus 'erasing' the pesky aerial from the shot. This 'glass matte', we were told, was a fairly common process dating back to the silent era. It was as old as Percy Quayle himself.

But Percy didn't seem angry or bitter about the glass matte. He didn't look like someone about to punch out an angry turd. He stood there, transfixed, like a curious kitten mesmerised by a dangling piece of string. It was a look I knew well. As with Skippy's fake paws and the Gemini Man's malfunctioning watch, Percy was in the process of realising that much of what we thought we were seeing on the goggle-box was, in fact, something else entirely. Something of dreams.

mono

Who needs a nickname when your real name is James Bond? There was a James Bond at my school, three years behind me. That means he was born in about 1967. That means his parents, unless they'd been living in a cave, had known exactly what they were doing. Sentencing him to a lifetime of hell. And at no time would the flames be hotter than during that first year of high school. From the moment he stepped off the bus for Day One of Form Three, James Bond was fucked.

There were the obvious jokes. At lunchtime he was, of course, both shaken and stirred. There were the endless requests that he say 'Bond . . . James Bond' in what was a most unfortunate halting falsetto. And needless to say, the title *Goldfinger* afforded many an opportunity for creative toilet humour. I myself got onto the score-board in the very first week when, in my capacity as a New Stationery Monitor, I found myself face-to-face with the elusive Mr Bond. After heroically resisting the chance to have him repeat his name, I reached under the counter and produced his already-assembled bag of first-year stationery.

'This is for English, and you'll need two of these for Maths.'

I explained the exercise books, just as they had been explained to me three years earlier.

'And this is your pen,' I said, holding up a standard blue Bic Biro. 'At least, it *looks* like a pen, 007 . . .' But before I could get to the good bit he'd snatched it from me and fled like . . . well, like James Bond.

All fairly predictable, I suppose, but the finest and most creative moments came courtesy of Monty Norman's famous 'James Bond Theme'. It seemed everyone in the school could do it and the familiar stings would accompany almost any action or movement from Bond, particularly during phys. ed. or at the pool. If he happened to walk past a class waiting in a corridor, the entire line would break into the legendary guitar motif. If he tried to make a run for it, the theme would speed up with him. Most classes had it down, with the various instruments divided up between them. The most spectacular mass rendition occurred one Friday morning when James was forced to walk onto the stage during assembly to receive some sort of handshake from the deputy principal. Unfortunately for him, he was seated at the very back of the assembly hall. By the time he reached the podium, nine hundred students and several teachers were already up to the first bridge. I'm sure James saw the funny side.

I'd love to report that the young Bond met a sticky end one day in metalwork when a giant laser sliced him in two, but sadly, this was not to be. After a year and a half, he simply moved away, presumably to kick-start the very same jokes all over again in a different climate. A private school up north had stolen our muse, and I longed to hear what fresh variations they would contrive. No bulletins were forthcoming, but I'm sure they came up with some great material of their own, especially when *Octopussy* was given the green light.

I was one of the lucky ones. I made it through four-and-a-half years of high school without attracting a single nickname. As 'Tony' was already a bastardisation of 'Anthony', no further work was deemed necessary. And because my own rather high-pitched voice and Gandhiesque physique — my 'yardglass figure', as I called it — provided enough raw material for the required generation of cruelties, my fortunately nondescript name emerged unmutilated. I might also note that by the late 1970s, very few people remembered the Tony Martin who, as one reviewer put it, 'ruined' the Marx Brothers' film *The Big Store*, so I avoided finding myself on the receiving end of a James Bond-style vendetta.

One of the best nicknames I ever heard belonged to a gentleman I once worked with who, despite being universally loved, had absolutely no chin. He was known, although never to his face, such as it was, as 'Tontine'. After several weeks, someone finally explained it to me: without a chin, it's very difficult to fit a pillowcase.

That level of craftsmanship was never in evidence at any of my schools. I remember there was a kid who everyone used to call 'The Tool'. I admired that it was always 'The Tool', rather than just 'Tool', but it was still nothing to write home about. There were two 'Dongers', two 'Tuggers', one 'Sprog' and a boy called Dick Bolger, whose rather superfluous nickname was 'Pants'.

At one school, there was a French–Canadian boy by the name of Brendan Canut. Canut was actually pronounced 'canoe', but everyone insisted on calling him 'K-Nut', which was considered so brilliant that it caught on, and 'K-Nut' graffiti started appearing on school property, and the deputy principal had to make a plea at assembly for the 'K-Nut madness to end'. My friend Kelly Dwyer had a sister called Barbara, and I pointed out that if she married Brendan Canut, her name would be 'Barb Dwyer-Canoe', but the 'K-Nut'-obsessed populace refused to accept my pronunciation and the joke fell on deaf ears.

Perhaps the only decent nickname coined at any school I attended was that of 'Mono', the boy with one testicle.

I can remember virtually nothing of what I was taught in Geography, Maths or Chemistry, but I recall with blinding clarity the assertion that Hitler had only one big – or, in some cultures, brass – ball. The sonnet, as you may recollect, paints a picture of the Third Reich in various stages of testicular disrepair. It suggests that the Führer's lonely gonad provided him with little solace during those final days in the bunker, but that at least he had been spared the fate of 'poor old Goebbels'.

This was the ditty I instinctively started to hum as word went around the playground at Thames South that Dale Tallboy, the weird religious kid, had only one big ball. I think it was big. It certainly wasn't brass. Whatever it was, it was supposedly unaccompanied. From where, and how, this information had been obtained was never made clear, and no actual eyewitness accounts were ever tabled, but the rumour gathered steam and by about lunchtime, Dale Tallboy had been rechristened 'Mono'.

'Mono!' they'd shout as they zipped past him in the bike-stands.

'Hey, Mono! Pocketing a single?'

Mono would just look at the ground and keep walking. He never once answered back. I'm telling you, the ball on that guy.

The Tallboys belonged to one of those religions with the word 'Brethren' in the name, where everything's as it was 200 years ago, except they're quite happy to drive around in cars. Mono wasn't really supposed to fraternise with the other kids – the heathens, as it were – and he walked to and from school alone. My enormous friend Colin Plympton and I were among the few he hung out with at lunchtime, possibly because we were the only ones who weren't shouting 'Mono!' at him all day. Mind you, we were thinking it. I was shocked to learn that Mono and his sister were forbidden by their parents to watch TV or go to the movies. It was sick and I told him so in no uncertain terms. I took great delight in corrupting him with talk of bionic arms and monkeys who drank cups of tea. Before long he could name every captive of *Gilligan's Island* without ever having seen an episode.

One time, after several entreaties by Mrs Plympton to the Tallboys, Mono was allowed to come round to Colin's for a barbecue, provided there would be no television or Satan worship. Colin's dad made a big show of putting a sheet over the TV set and pantomimed a search for evidence of diabolism. A packet of Little Lucifers was removed from view. We had worded everyone up about the whole 'Mono' thing, and although Mr Plympton found it hilarious and spent the next hour singing 'One is the Loneliest Number', all agreed not to bring it up and to try to remember to call him Dale.

'One is the loneliest —'

'Dad! You're not going to be singing that when he gets here, are you?'

'I hope not, Colin, but it's stuck in my head now.'

'Dad, this is Mono.'

Colin had fucked it up from the get-go.

'Sorry, *Dale*. It's Dale.'

'Nice to meet you, Dale. Heard a lot about you.'

Dale winced at the thought.

'Colin says you're religious.'

After a painfully extended silence, Dale held up the gift he was carrying, a flat object wrapped in brown paper.

'What's this?'

'It's a present from my parents.'

Colin's dad tore the paper off what appeared to be a breadboard.

'Very thoughtful, Dale. Did your dad make this himself?' Dale shook his head.

'No? Well, that's very interesting. So you're allowed to go to shops, then?'

'Dad!'

'All right, no offence. Jeez.'

Mr Plympton wandered off to the kitchen,

shaking his head and hugging his breadboard. Colin and I pondered our next move. With TV and comics forbidden, board games seemed the only option.

'Dale, do you know how to play Mouse Trap?'

'Not allowed to play Mouse Trap.'

'What's wrong with Mouse Trap?'

'It . . . promotes bad values,' said Dale in a way that suggested he found it as ridiculous as we did.

'Mouse Trap promotes bad values?' scoffed Colin, as we climbed the stairs.

'How can that be?' I said. 'You're just catching mice, that's all. In a very roundabout way.'

'Is it the boot?' queried Colin. 'The man on the diving board?'

'Is it the cheese?'

It was a stumper, all right. Bad values? It was only 'A Game of Zany Action on a Crazy Contraption'. This was years before Grand Theft Auto III.

We dragged all the games down from the hall cupboard, but none was deemed appropriate. Dale's eyes widened at the dazzling parade of colourful boxes, Drag Strip, Ker-Plunk, Hungry Hungry Hippos and the rest. But apparently their surrealistic imagery (snakes, ladders, etc), so far removed from everyday life, was nothing less than the Devil's work. Even The Game of Life itself was pronounced unlifelike, so we gave up. Only entertainments that reflected utterly the tone and realism of everyday life were acceptable to those of the Tallboys' faith.

Sadly, we had no 16mm prints of the work of John Cassavetes on hand, not at that barbecue, anyway, so that pretty much left nothing but . . . conversation. Bugger that.

'What are you boys doing inside? You should be outside, soaking in the sun's deadly rays.'

Those weren't Mrs Plympton's exact words, as this was the seventies and the sun was still our friend. But it was the 'What are you doing in here in the dark on such a bright and sunny day?' speech that we nerds dealt with on a daily basis.

Colin ran through our current repertoire of outside games: War, Sniper, Go Home Stay Home. Or we could do you Stuck in the Mud, Straight Chasey, Invisible Man or Everything in Reverse. Clearly, Everything in Reverse was not going to meet the required standards of realism and neither were any of the previous selections. Colin mounted a lengthy defence of the naturalism of Sniper, but as snipers were, in those days, unheard-of in the suburbs, that too was rejected. Even Making Your Way Around The Entire Property Standing Only On Things Made Of Concrete, although realistic in that it would have actually been happening, was dismissed on the grounds that it was both unlikely and unnecessary. These Brethren were tough nuts to crack.

Dale wasn't trying to be difficult. He seemed kind of embarrassed as he reeled off the objections like he'd done it a hundred times before. We asked him to suggest a game and he described something from the approved list, where you all sit in a circle and outline your goals in regard to making the world a better place to live in.

'All right, Dale,' I conceded. 'We'll play your little game. Everyone in a circle. Right, I'll go first. My goal is to live in a world where *you can play Mouse Trap*! Whaddaya reckon, Dale? Will you help me achieve my goal?'

Dale cracked and agreed to one round of Mouse Trap, so long as he could turn away when the cage finally dropped. But Colin's mum refused to let us back into the house, so there went that idea.

By this time Mr Plympton had ripped the tarp off the barbie and was setting up his tools of trade. The tinny outside speakers were squirting out some James Last Greek pastiche. Mr P had combed through the record selection to make sure there were no 'One is the Loneliest Number's lying coiled to embarrass us. 'S.S.S.Single Bed' was weeded out, as was 'Beside You I Have Nothing'.

Dale ate and drank exactly like the rest of us, and I noticed he hoved into the plate of Animal Biscuits, despite their flagrant unrealism. Once we were all perched on the outdoor furniture, balancing our leaking snag sandwiches, Colin's dad resumed his subtle interrogation of the alien.

'So, Dale, what do your mum and dad do?'
'Dad works at the car factory.'
'Right . . .'

We knew it was coming.

'So cars are allowed, then?'

'Dad!'

'Nah, hear me out. I just wanna know why some things like TV are out and yet modern things like factories are allowed.'

It should be mentioned that, by now, Mr P had had a few. But Dale remained calm and had an answer prepared.

'It's not the TV, Mr Plympton, it's what's on the TV,' he explained.

'Right, I get it, Dale. And fair enough too. You should see the rubbish these two watch all bloody day, if you'll excuse my pagan tongue.'

Now Mr P. was in Dale's corner.

'Bloody robots and time tunnels and whatnot. I try to get them to watch the news, but they say it's boring. How can real life be boring, Dale? You know what I'm talking about. But no, unless it's got bloody mod squads and cybernauts and all that carry-on, they're not interested. Maybe I should come and move in with your lot. You seem to have your head screwed on right.'

Dale looked mortified by the idea of Colin's dad living with the Tallboys.

'Ooh, hang on, is alcohol allowed?'

Dale shook his head.

'I'll be staying here, then.'

'Dale, your dad's here.'

Dale had to go. It had been exactly one hour. We

all raced for the front door to see what his dad looked like.

Mr Tallboy was a regular-looking dad in normal dad clothes. He wasn't dressed in pants with a rope belt and wasn't driving a horse and buggy. He wasn't smoking a corn cob pipe and didn't have a beard like a leprechaun. He shook hands with us all and may even have cracked a joke. It was most odd.

The Tallboys left in their normal-looking station wagon and Colin's dad just stood there, looking as confused as the rest of us. It was a full twenty seconds before he spoke.

'Did you see his watch? It was like an underwater sports watch. So obviously they're allowed.'

'And they're allowed underwater,' I added.

''Cos that's real,' said Colin.

'I dunno,' said Colin's dad, staring into the middle distance. 'They didn't seem that religious to me.'

Eventually, the Tallboys became comfortable enough with the Plymptons to allow Mono to spend an entire Saturday afternoon round at Colin's. The stated plan was that Dale, Colin and myself would be going on a bushwalk, up where the houses stopped and the hills continued. But this was a subterfuge. It had taken weeks, but Colin and I had convinced Dale to accompany us to a Saturday matinee at the pictures. Dale was nearly ten and had never seen a movie. This simply wouldn't do.

Dale hadn't even seen television. The language of cinema, the cutting, the camera angles, the music . . .

everything would be new to him. Colin and I would discover the magic of movies all over again, through someone else's eyes. It was the primary school equivalent of getting someone laid. But what film to choose for this poor one-balled movie virgin? What masterpiece would we select? *2001: A Space Odyssey*? *The Seventh Seal*? *Psycho*?

'Tony, there's a sequel to *The Computer Wore Tennis Shoes*!'

Colin and I had been big fans of the first Dexter Riley film, with the young Kurt Russell as the plucky college kid who accidentally becomes superintelligent and makes the headmaster look like an idiot.

'In this one he accidentally becomes invisible!'

'This is it! This is the one we've been waiting for!'

It was clear from the ad in the *Thames Star* that *Now You See Him, Now You Don't* wasn't going to be a major work of neo-realism. But invisibility! How could Dale say no to that? The concept of invisibility was one of the few flights of fancy on which he allowed himself to join us. Over a series of lunchtime thinktanks, the three of us had agreed that invisibility was the most desirable of the super powers, for all the obvious, prurient reasons. Now Dexter Riley himself would provide us with a firsthand demonstration of what it would be like to possess such awesome power. Colin noted, with some disappointment, that the movie was rated 'G'.

Dale was visibly stunned when the man tore his

ticket in half. I consoled him with the manner of an old hand at the Saturday matinee game.

'Strap yourself in, Dale,' I said slipping the half-ticket into his trembling paw. 'It gets a lot hairier from hereon in.'

The Thames Embassy was probably a fleapit, but it was where I wanted to spend the rest of my life. Dale was visibly blown away.

'It's like . . . it's like a church,' he gasped.

Colin and I nodded sagely and stroked our invisible beards.

As always, the back row was filled, so we took three aisle seats, two-thirds of the way back in the upstairs. Dale was fascinated by the advertising slide show, already in progress, and when the curtains closed and opened again and the lights started to go down, he froze, halfway through his box of chocolate Snifters.

The documentary was so boring that only Dale enjoyed it. *Our Friend Salt* ran for forty minutes and by the end, both Colin and I were noisily feigning sleep. The cartoon was a 'Road Runner', and Dale was so disturbed we had to take him down to the foyer only one minute in. It was strange to see someone exhibit so much compassion for such an evil coyote.

But the feature went down a storm. *Now You See Him, Now You Don't* was, as expected, a work of genius. The Dexter Riley team had outdone themselves. They'd set the bar so high it would take them three years to produce the follow-up, *The Strongest Man in the World*. Dale roared at the jokes and, like us, took squealing delight in the headmaster's paint-splattered come-uppance. The climactic chase featured Dexter and co. wreaking havoc in an invisible car, and when they drove across a rickety wooden bridge, pitching mystified fishermen into the drink in their invisible wake, I thought Dale, and indeed all of us, would never be able to walk again. That entire sequence brought the house down, though in retrospect, we all agreed that how they managed to spray the invisible spray on the invisible spray gun itself was never adequately explained.

As we clambered our way home up a creek, Dale admitted that yes, he had enjoyed himself and that no, he hadn't been damaged for life. *Now You See Him, Now You Don't* was clearly all just pretend. No-one had been hurt, those fishermen would have recovered, and the evil Dean Higgins probably wasn't evil at all in real life.

We never again got Mono to a movie, and I often wonder if he ever saw another one. Imagine if the only movie you ever saw was *Now You See Him, Now You Don't*.

About a year later, Mr Tallboy's religion dictated that he move to Australia and open a pub. Our final conversation with Dale was on the last day of school. We said goodbye, as ten-year-olds do, in high voices, looking at the ground. Other boys sent him off in the only way they knew how. 'Mono! How's it hangin'?'

During the two years we knew him, neither Colin nor I once asked Dale about the whole 'Mono' thing. We wouldn't have known how. Behind his back we, like the others, made our own one-ball jokes, but these were abstract and private. Mono was our friend, a fresh impartial audience for our time-tunnel theories and, to us, an endless source of novelty, what with his bizarre insistence on living in the real world.

Months after the Tallboys' departure, Colin and I received some baffling news. Word started going around that while Mono had been at Thames South, he'd been involved in a sports accident. During a game of pegball, a stray swung bat had struck him fair in the genital. We'd heard about this, but what we didn't know was that Dale had been rushed to Sick Bay, where the nurse had examined him and discovered that he did in fact possess two, somewhat swollen, testicles.

We were gobsmacked. If this was true, why had he gone along with the whole 'Mono' thing? Was not the fame of being the weird religious kid enough? Did the tedium of his realist existence require that he encourage this rumour, or at least not discourage it, so that he might have one secret illusion of his own? A single drop of one-balled fancy in a life otherwise utterly grounded in the double-nadded scrotum of reality?

Then again, perhaps to live with the slur was easier than having to offer up proof of its falseness. I could understand that.

'But couldn't he have told *us*?' asked Colin. 'Let *us* in on the secret?'

Just as we had dragged him into our world of fantasy, Dale had involved us in one of his own. A believable one. The fantasy that he was one ball short. And we bought it. We all bought it.

Dale Tallboy. No TV, no movies, but a wild imagination.

I hear that Himmler had something sim'lar.

longnecks

It was a whole street full of solo mums. There was Kieran Soandso and her two mental boys at the brown flats on the corner; Miss Traven and her sorry lot at the hostel next door, where they couldn't afford to fill the pool; my mum, me and my asthmatic half-brother at the flat with the nutty green carport; and on the other side, the always-out Mrs Brazier, whose eldest, Duane, once came home in a police car, and she had to get old Harry Penman from down the back to give him the strap. Harry was too polite to say no and did agree that somebody had to do it. Actual dads were pretty thin on the ground, and benefit cheques snowed from the letterboxes every second Tuesday.

This was where I found myself living after my mother's latest successful divorce in the mid-to-late seventies. Hillcrest, Hamilton, home of the Hillcrest Tavern, home of a covers band that only covered other covers bands, just over the back fence and round the corner from the badminton centre, where, if you were really bored – and why wouldn't you be? – you could call reception, just to hear the lady say:

'Badmin Admin?'

'What?'

'I said Badmin Admin.'

'Why would you say that?'

'I'm sorry, who is this?'

'Say it again.'

'What?'

'Badmin Admin.'

'I'm going to hang up now.'

'What, and go back to work at Badmin Admin?'

Click.

It was my third Badmin Admin call of the afternoon and already I was bored. Our four-room flat was small, but with high ceilings and windows all down the front, which sent sunlight spilling into every corner, where usually you'd find a cat or a Mills & Boon. Mum was in Auckland for the day visiting her half-relatives, and my brother Michael Different-Surname was on his court-enforced fortnightly stay with his dad, formerly my step-dad – not my real dad, who was, at that time, off being the dad of my other half-brother, whom I'd never met. The family tree was getting out of control. The council had twice asked us to prune it back.

But that Tuesday afternoon during one school holiday or another, I was on my own. Just me, the cats and the carport, that ridiculous carport. I stood on the front steps in my fraying-roped dressing gown, eating sultanas from a tiny carton, and tried to remember where the hell the carport had come from. It was basically a steel frame covered in green panels of light corrugated plastic, anchored to the ground with tentpegs, and wedged against the front of the house in full view of passing, rightfully appalled, neighbours. Even though my mother's car was possibly the smallest four-wheeled vehicle on sale in New Zealand – the Fiat 500 Bambina – it only had about ten centimetres of leeway on either side of the 'shell'. It was a giant ribbed plastic condom and piloting the Bambina into it could take up to ten full minutes. One time Belinda, one of the students from Flat 2, borrowed Mum's car and was halfway down the drive before she realised the side mirror had snagged the frame, and that the car was 'wearing' the carport out. The thing was so light, I dragged it back to the house myself. Every time I dared point out to my mother that our laughable green annex was lowering the tone of our already tone-lowered block, she would insist that its very inaccessibility was what made our car an unlikely target for thieves. That well-organised car thieves would be unlikely to target a mustard-coloured Bambina with no muffler, unless desperate, insane or keen to be involved in the funniest car chase of all time, seemed not to have occurred to her. But I guess she had a point. Extricating the Bambina would require nothing less than the steady hand of a master safecracker.

'Nice carport.' It was Noel, boyfriend of Donna, who babysat for Mrs Brazier next door. Blue beanie, green Swanndri, tracky dacks and Doc Martens. An unlit cigarette a-dangle and a light brown moustache trying hard to be taken seriously.

'You seen Donna?'

'I don't think she's on today.'

'Said she was. Said she'd be here all day.'

He granted the cigarette a reprieve and returned it, carefully, to the pack.

'You see 'em go out?'

'Nup'.

'Mind if I wait here?'

'Um . . .'

'Got to get somethin' from the car.' He headed back to his mud-sealed ute, which was angled across Mrs Brazier's front lawn amidst three other vehicles, only one of which had wheels. It was a flophouse for old Valiants.

One minute later he lurched into our sun-blasted loungeroom clutching a brown paper bag, the contents of which he was so keen to get at that there was no time for the doormat. He wiped his boots one at a time on the legs of his pants in a mad, stumbling hop-dash for the dining room table.

'Got an opener?' he said, producing two longnecks of DB with a conjurer's finesse. As I made for the kitchen to detach the bottle-opener from its string, Noel laid out the two tall bottles, sat down and began examining them as though he'd just paid a thousand dollars for each at Sotheby's.

'Old enough to join me?' he enquired.

I shook my head.

'Well, don't mind me, it's just that time of the afternoon,' he explained, knocking the top off not one, but both, bottles. He poured part of one into a Ribena glass, and left the other to stand.

'You want me to put that in the fridge?' I asked.

'Nah, mate,' he shot back. 'They're right there where I can see 'em.'

Within seconds his moustache fronds were tipped with beer froth and a satisfied intake of breath revealed him to be one of those people with more gum than tooth. It was like his gums were slowly descending over his teeth, enveloping them like gum-cuticles, leaving only the fine points of the teeth poking through. After every mouthful of beer he would top up his glass from the bottle. It looked like a lot of fun. I went to the fridge and poured myself a lime cordial from the plastic jug.

'So what's the set-up here?'

'How do you mean?'

'Just you and your mum, is it?'

'And my brother.'

'Where's he?'

'Staying with his dad.'

'Oh, right. I getcha. Your dad?'

'His.'

'Right. Where's yours?'

'According to Mum, he's off... what's the word?'

'Pissed?'

'Gallivanting.'

'Oh, right. Gallivanting.' He repeated it, like he was trying it on for size. 'Few more of these and I might be on for a "gallivant" meself.'

He took another swig and topped up the glass.

'I'm putting the TV on,' I announced.

'Hey, yeah – see if the cricket's on.'

Cricket. The most boring sport in the world, aside from all the other ones. I wearily ignited the set, and soon the ping-pong natter of cricket commentary was wafting from the single oval speaker.

'Not into it?'

'Not really.'

'Switch over, if you want. Just wanted the score.'

I switched over. More cricket, then ads. Noel spoke the very words I was thinking.

'Ever since we got this second channel, there's twice as much shit on, don't you reckon?'

'There's some good things. I like *Oh No, It's Selwyn Froggitt*.'

He stared at me like I'd made the title up. But I hadn't. He turned and focussed on the TV, which was now playing a promo for *The Sweeney*. 'Fuckin' cops!' he suddenly spat. At *The Sweeney*. 'Where do you reckon Donna's gone? She can't have gone too far with them kids.'

'I don't know. Haven't seen her all day.'

'Uh-huh.'

He seemed to be considering his next line very carefully. 'You ever see her with any other guys?'

'While she's babysitting?'

'She ever have anyone else drop by?'

'I haven't seen anyone.'

'Right.' For a few seconds he stared at the TV. Then he said: 'So what do *you* think's goin' on with her?'

'Going on? *I* dunno. She's just looking after the kids.'

'On her own?'

'When you're not there.' Which he was every second day, it seemed.

'When I'm . . . not . . . there,' he said, one word at a time. Then, after another shot of DB . . . 'What do *you* think of her?'

'Donna?'

'Yeah. She's all right, isn't she?'

'She's nice.'

'Yeah, she is,' he concurred. 'She is nice. And she's got a great arse.'

This I ignored, as it would have been unseemly to

endorse such a vulgar remark about Donna. For, although she didn't know it yet, I was madly in love with her.

At least, that's what I thought at the time. I was fourteen, what did I know about love? Going by our family, love was something that inevitably ended in court proceedings. It was something to be avoided at all costs. Unless you wanted to get smacked around.

But eighteen-year-old Donna Keely was, in the words of her twenty-nine-year-old boyfriend, 'as cute as a damn button'. Often, when speaking of her, Noel would intone this mantra, artfully dropping the 'as cute'. 'As a *damn* button,' he'd say, shaking his head in wonderment.

She was tall and dark-haired and long-limbed and had a look in her eye that suggested she might be on for anything. She clearly had Noel under some kind of spell and, from what I could see, she did it by ignoring him. By keeping him guessing. By playing with his mind. Because that's what she was doing with me. Well, mostly the first part. The ignoring.

The spell was also maintained via a series of outfits that always elicited the same single-word description from my mother: inappropriate. But I was going to a boys' school. As far as I was concerned, the more inappropriate, the better.

Donna was my kind of babysitter, all right, but I wasn't fool enough to think that anything might come of it. After all, she was Noel's girl, even though, to me, he looked old enough to be her father. And just weird enough.

Noel was onto the second bottle. The time was right to start poking my nose into his and Donna's history.

'So how long have you two been going out?'

He had to think about it. 'Oooh, let's see. Five months, maybe six. Or four.'

'How did you meet?'

'She was working behind the counter at the manure stop.'

'The manure stop?'

'Where I work. On the road to Morrinsville. It's where people stop, for manure.'

'You work with manure?'

'I don't handle the manure myself. I'm the assistant manager. It's mostly paperwork.'

'And so Donna . . .'

'She was there for about three weeks. She didn't care for it.'

'No?'

'It's not for everyone, manure.'

Did it really seem that unlikely, a fourteen-year-old high school student with a tenuous grip on puberty being squired around town by an eighteen-year-old bombshell? Perhaps, but perhaps not when compared with an eighteen-year-old girl being romanced by a twenty-nine-year-old assistant shit-clerk in a turd-spattered ute, who would have been rejected by the casting director on *Deliverance* for looking 'too creepy'? 'Noel, can I ask . . . how do you do it?'

'What?'

'Get someone like Donna to go out with you?'

Noel expelled a breath that lasted at least five seconds. 'Tony, in spite of appearances, I'm not a dirty old man.'

A twenty-nine-year-old dirty old man. That would have been the perfect description for him, had he not confounded expectations with the following admission.

'I'm a very polite person. Very old-fashioned.'

'Yeah?'

'I like to observe the niceties.'

'Like, how?'

'Well, you've just gotta open doors when required. Buy her stuff. Make sure she's well taken care of, in *all* departments. It's not rocket science.'

Thankfully not. I don't think they'd have allowed the drinking.

'Courtesy. Politeness. They still teachin' them at school?'

'No, but there is something new called "Media Studies".'

'The ladies still respond to the old ways, Tony. You can write that down.'

'Well, I'm sure boys'd be interested in courtesy if they were to see . . .'

The sentence realised where it was going and pulled over.

'See what?' he asked. 'Me girl?'

'Er . . . yeah.'

'You a bit keen on her yourself, are you?'

My face had turned the exact colour of Cheech & Chong's *Sleeping Beauty* album.

'She'd eat you for breakfast, buddy.'

It was a breakfast I'd have been happy to attend.

There had been only one occasion where I'd been able to get anywhere near the orbit of Donna Keely. It was a hot, cicada-buzzing, daylight-saved Wednesday evening round seven, and Mrs B. and Duane were out of town, leaving Heather, aged eight, and Niall, ten, in Donna's long and capable hands. This, I felt, would be a good time to pop over and return some of Duane's comics. In truth, they were mine, two sub-standard issues of *Green Lantern* I was glad to be rid of. For Duane was someone I generally avoided. He stank of trouble. He'd once asked me to hide a brand-new briefcase under my bed for a few days. After he'd gone, I opened it. It was empty. Another time he got me to answer his front door and tell the man that no, Duane Brazier doesn't live here anymore, I think he's moved to Auckland. One day he gave me some wire-cutters and challenged me to steal the stapler from the post office. I couldn't do it and returned with only a fistful of deposit slips and a refill from one of the chained-down Biros.

Donna answered the door in something outrageously inappropriate.

'What?'

'These uh . . . these comics . . . they're mine.'

Fuck!

'I mean, they're Duane's. I'm bringing them.'

Not bringing them *back*, just bringing them.

'Do you want to come in?'

'Yeah. Yes. Yep.'

She laughed and gestured towards the sunroom. 'They're in there. Do you want a hot dog?'

'I'll yes.'

I'll yes?

'Go through.'

I went through, to discover Heather and Niall playing the Escape From Colditz board game on the floor. Each was holding a polony wrapped in bread and they were both dripping tomato sauce onto the board.

'Duane's looking for you,' said Niall, without looking up.

Great. Maybe this time I'll get to blow something up.

'I've brought his comics back.' There was no need to have said that. I was already in. But the kids didn't hear me, anyway.

'All the bits are over there,' said Donna, pointing me towards the snags, the bread and the tomato sauce. Then she picked up the phone and resumed a breathless conversation. 'Y'there? So what *was* the reason? You're shitting me!'

The Braziers' phone had a long, long cord and Donna sauntered barefoot around the sunroom, occasionally looking across to me as she nodded intently at some of the more scandalous revelations. 'You cannot be serious! Why? Why would she be there on the exact same night? Well, what did *you* say? And what did *he* say? Oh, that is *stink*!'

Inadvisably, I returned one of her glances with a goonish eyebrows-raised smile, as if to say, 'Sounds like one crazy phone call!' For a moment, I thought she was going to hang up and call the police, but it was just a particularly serious bit.

'I wouldn't stand for that. I'd give him what-for.'

I finished my unstable, over-sauced refreshment as suavely as I could and made a second attempt to engage Niall. Somehow I had to prolong my visit until Donna got off the phone. 'So, where is Duane?'

'Gone somewhere.'

'Right. And your mum?'

'Yep.'

I had another card to play.

'So . . . youse gonna be watching *M*A*S*H*?'

'When's it on?'

'Now.'

LOLLY SCRAMBLE

Niall scrambled for the TV and punched it on. By the time he got over to the couch, the screen was a sea of olive drab, broken only by Klinger's latest canary-yellow ensemble. Equally hypnotised, Heather climbed up next to her brother, followed craftily by me. Now I had a reason to be there. *M*A*S*H* was on. Soon we'd all be reeling at the antics of the men and women of the 4077th, and Donna would have no choice but to join us.

But there was something disturbingly different about this episode. With a creeping sense of horror I realised that it was one of the ones directed by Alan Alda himself. One of the ones where it went all serious and there was heaps more blood and no laugh track. It was like an Ingmar Bergman film but with fewer jokes. Heather lost interest within thirty seconds and stomped off to her room. Niall and I endured the gore and the earnestness, and the discovery that it was all a dream, until the end credits — which may have run in silence — kicked in and released us from our considerable misery. Even at that early age I wondered what Robert Altman thought of this grotesque mockery of his original 1970 film, which, of course, I hadn't seen. In fact, I'd never seen a single Robert Altman film, only read about them in the old copies of *Sight & Sound* at the Hamilton Public Library.

Miraculously, Donna was still gasping and saying 'No!' on the phone and had been spared the entire travesty. But as the credits ended, she interrupted her flow of gaping disbelief to order Niall to 'Get the bed ready.' The ten-year-old waved me off the couch which, with a flurry of well-practised moves, he somehow folded out into a double bed, ready-furnished with a huge 'Holly Hobby' eiderdown.

Then, as the cheesecake avalanche that was the opening credits of *Charlie's Angels* began to roll, the three of them sprang into action. Donna immediately told her informant, 'Gotta go,' and with one dazzlingly lithe gambol, flew across the room and bounced onto the bed, taking up centre position. Niall burrowed in beside her, and the now pyjama-clad Heather appeared from nowhere and threw herself against Donna's vacant side. This was apparently a regular ritual.

'Wanna watch *Charlie's Angels*?' said Donna, with a look that suggested she had no idea who I was.

'Sure!' I said, with unnecessary volume.

'Up here,' she said, indicating the space next to Heather.

My heart instantly skipped two grooves. Technically, Donna Keely was asking me to come to bed with her. Sure, we were both fully clothed and there were two other minors present, but it was a bed and she was inviting me to join her on it, to watch something which at least one newspaper editorial had declared to be 'pornography'. I clambered onto my spot feeling very odd indeed. Even though there was an eight-year-old between us, this was probably the closest I'd ever been to a fully grown girl I wasn't related, half-related or step-related to. Donna's long, nut-brown legs splayed out across the bed, and they, rather than the Angels, who were by now well into their Cheryl Ladd period, commanded my attention.

It was fashionable at that time to enquire of friends and colleagues, 'Who's your favourite Angel?' and I prayed that I would be spared the embarrassment of that question during what was fast becoming a hormonal crisis.

'Tony, who's your favourite Angel?'

The shock of the question was more than tempered by the realisation that she did actually know my name. 'Um . . . I don't like the new one,' I squeaked.

'*That's* not an answer,' she teased, revelling in my discomfort.

'Farrah Fawcett!' yelled Niall.

'No, let him answer,' said Donna, hitting Niall with a pillow.

'She's not in it anymore,' I said, still hedging.

'Come *on-n-n*,' she sang.

In fact, I didn't particularly care for any of them. I didn't become a regular viewer until years later, when Tanya Roberts joined the cast. 'Jaclyn Smith,' I finally announced, prompting shrill mocking sirens from all three.

'You *love* her. You *love* Jaclyn Smith,' insisted Niall.

'Interesting,' pondered Donna. 'I would have guessed either Kate Jackson or Bosley.'

That was it. They were gone. The bed was awash with tormenting hysterics and I had no comeback, nothing. The ad break arrived and I quietly said my goodbyes. All three struggled to maintain a straight face. As I reached the door, Donna used my name again. 'Tony . . .'

I turned. 'Yes?'

'Don't forget your comics.'

Noel was laughing so hard that beer was coming out of his nose. 'Fuckin' hell!' he gasped. 'That's her. That's her, all right.'

I don't know why I'd told him the whole story. Maybe it was the lime cordial talking.

'You gotta have one of these, bud,' he said, pouring me a tiny beer. 'And here's a tip for you. Anyone gives you the "Which Angel?" question, the correct answer is: "All three . . . at once!"'

He cracked himself up. I just sat there and imagined myself doing the line. I knew immediately I could never pull it off. It would be years before I could say it. Years before I even *understood* it. I took a sip of beer. It tasted like salt water.

The bottles were empty, and not a moment too soon. Noel was on his feet and fumbling for his keys. 'Well, listen, if you see her, tell her I was here, but don't mention any of what I said, all right?'

Like I was going to repeat the 'great arse' line.

'Seeya, bud.' He stumbled off to the ute, leaving me with the empties.

I was awoken by the sound of a backfiring Bambina. Mum was back early! The half-glass of beer had knocked me out cold . . . and the two empty bottles were still sitting on the dining room table. *Shit!* Must act quickly! She was reversing into the carport. I had only ten full minutes to hide the bottles.

the secret passage

'Will someone tell the corpses to keep it down!'

Herb Rafter, like many stage managers I would encounter, had the ability to shout at full volume, in a whisper. He could yell at you from the wings and somehow the front row of the audience didn't hear a thing. He was like a Gatling gun with a silencer.

The 'corpses' were the characters in the play who'd already been killed off, and on this night they were especially boisterous. It was the second-to-last performance and the final night piss-up was, for them, just one extended death scene away.

'Take that racket outside, you lot. There's people up here still waiting to be murdered.'

The living dead wandered out the back with a warm cask of wine, all still in costume, as the curtain call was coming up and everyone was under instructions to 'keep themselves nice'. This was because 'we don't want a repeat of what happened with *'Tis a Pity She's Dismembered* a couple of years back'.

What exactly had happened with *'Tis*, as they referred to it, was information I was not yet privy to. I was too far down the ladder. I had just turned eighteen and this was my first job in the theatre. The amateur theatre, that is, or rather, the 'non-professional theatre', as I had been instructed to call it at all times. And this was regional non-professional light comedy theatre at its very best. The Peppercorn Players celebrating their umpteenth successful year with a crowd-pleasing romp from the acclaimed author of *Headless at the Vicarage*.

And there was my name in the programme, listed second under 'stage crew', right after my oldest friend Keith Delwyn's name – which was, in keeping with an old amateur theatre tradition, spelt incorrectly. This was unfair, as it was Keith who had secured me the job. If anyone deserved to be misspelt it was me, the greenhorn. I was also disappointed with the plain heading 'stage crew'. I had hoped to see my name accompanied by a more accurate description of my actual task: operating the secret door. Or, as Herb put it, 'Trying not to fuck up'.

You Screamed, M'Lord? is one of those British farces where a whole lot of eccentric toffs gather at a remote country house one stormy evening for the reading of a will. You can guess the rest. The play's fully justified opportunities for enormous accents and endlessly milkable death scenes meant that Peppercorn's production was one of eight being staged by New Zealand dramatic societies that year. Eight! This one play was responsible for over 500 grisly fictional deaths over a fourteen-month period, refreshments included.

It's hard to think of the right word to describe the old Peppercorn Theatre. 'Firetrap' barely does it justice. 'An army barracks full of poofs' was a description my only openly homosexual friend once used, and he was partly right. About thirty per cent right, which for AmDram is standard, in my experience.

There was nothing gay, in either sense of the word, about Herb Rafter. He was like Lawrence Tierney on a particularly bad day. His three backstage rules were:

1. Don't pester the actors.
2. Be quiet.
3. Shut the fuck up.

And foolish was the man who attempted to point out that numbers 2 and 3 were kind of the same thing. 'Wrong! As you'll soon discover!' he barked, his terracotta skull mere centimetres from my face.

Keith had wangled me onto Herb's crew after

wangling himself onto it for *Mine's a Biggun* earlier that year. On my very first day I dropped a tray of spoons backstage during rehearsal and Herb gave me a look that said, 'See? *That's* the difference.' I didn't see, though, as making a loud noise without actually speaking would, it seemed, still be covered by 'Shut the fuck up'. But there was no time to discuss this, as I could hear someone calling my name.

'Mr Martin, could you come out here, please?'

It was the director, a man overseeing his nineteenth production with Peppercorn in nineteen years. He was perfectly nice, but I still feared him as one would Erich Von Stroheim, had he been reduced to helming a regional production of *Not Now, Darling*.

Stepping out onto the tiny Peppercorn stage, I felt as thousands must have before me as they entered, stage right, to proclaim the emperor dead or announce to someone, 'Your husband's coming!' I stood amidst the half-painted plywood environs of 'Murdersby Manor' and gazed into the audience. An audience of one, but even so I was shitting myself. Imagine coming out to a full house – approx 150, including comps – with only the champagne dialogue of *You Screamed, M'Lord?* to protect you. Thank Christ I was going to be back there, behind the secret door.

'Mr Martin, do you think you could catch a valuable vase if someone were to throw it to you?'

'To me, or at me?'

'To you, from about six feet away?'

'Sure. Why not? Sounds like fun.'

'Well, we may have a very special job for you.'

Another one? Secret door-operating. Valuable vase-catching. This was a world away from my day job at the army surplus store. And, as all who partake know, that is the heady attraction of amateur dramatics. Forklift driver by day, King of Siam by night. That and the drinking.

In four years of non-professional amateur theatre, I learnt that if I'm going to fuck up, it's going to be during the second-to-last show. I think it's because the end is in sight and I simply let my guard down. The final night is fine, as that one is usually a festival of pranks and in-jokes and attempts to sabotage everyone else's carefully crafted work. This is not irresponsible behaviour or evidence that the company is not taking the work seriously, it is purely tradition, as old as the theatre itself. As long as there has been enacted storytelling there has been the surprise closing-night appearance of a performer's penis, unseen by the audience but visible to those on-stage.

'Why, yes, Lady Fortescue. As you can see, my credentials speak for themselves.'

But nothing ever happens on the second-to-last night. Unless you're working with me.

'Tony, can you mind the levels? I've got to move my car.'

Tom Baigent was in charge of sound and overlooked the stage from a tiny booth you had to crouch into, like a sniper's nest. It housed a milk crate to sit on, a mixing desk the size of a box of Cadbury Continentals and the massive reel-to-reel tape recorder which contained all the sound effects for the show, arranged sequentially, on one tape. There was dramatic music for the opening, then thunder and lightning, a doorbell, more thunder, two more doorbells and then, for Tom, a fifteen-minute wait before the next effect. That was where we were up to.

As Tom padded off to the carpark, I settled into his cocoon and pulled on the headphones. I knew how to listen to the effects in 'cue' so you could hear them in the phones, without broadcasting them through the PA. I shuttled through the second act – more doorbells, gramophone music, a scream with extra echo, a dog tearing at someone's trousers. I loved listening to sound effects and had, to the bemusement of my friends, invested in several of the famous BBC sound effects records. And not just the ones with gunshots and vomiting. I was impressed by how Tom, unhappy with the reverb on the BBC's 'Man Falling Down Stairs', had created his own superior version for a later scene where a character dies – to the dismay of the actor playing him – off-stage. I played the recording back in the headphones, over and over, trying to work out how he'd done it, how he'd timed all the extra tinkles and tin cans rolling off at the end. It was first-class. *Goon Show* quality.

Suddenly the headphones were wrenched off and I felt myself being hoisted from my seat.

Herb Rafter had me in a headlock. 'We've just heard "Man Falling Down Stairs" three times in a fucking row!' he whispered, at top volume. 'During the will reading! What the fuck is going on?'

'I was just . . . re-cueing the effects.'

'Why were they *un*-cued? Where's Tom?'

'Moving his car.'

'Stone the bloody crows! Aren't you meant to be catching that valuable vase in a minute?'

'Not 'til after Lady Whatsername gets shot.'

'Right – well, bloody get back down there. I'll fix this. Shoo.'

I passed Tom on the way down.

'Everything all right?'

'It's going well.'

That would probably have been enough cock-ups for one show, especially considering that nothing of any note had gone wrong during the entire two-week run. There had been only one, quickly corrected, instance of 'scene going round in circle', a well-covered 'late entrance due to problematic French windows', and the usual 'tea urn in foyer boiling loudly during quiet bit'. That was it. Even the guns had gone off, every night, on cue. There'd been no curtain trouble, and all the ham had been kept well within *You Screamed, M'Lord?*'s exceedingly generous parameters. As I recall, one character was a werewolf.

If something was going to go wrong, it was most likely to be the bit with the valuable vase. At one point in *You Screamed, M'Lord?*, a character is supposed to drop, and smash, a large antique vase, on-stage in full view of the audience. Farmer's department store had kindly furnished us with an extremely impressive china specimen, but only on the condition it be returned intact. The director's solution? The actor carrying the vase would trip and fling it through an open door into the wings, where I would catch it, in silence. At that exact moment Tom Baigent would trigger a 'vase smashing' sound effect and no-one would be any the wiser. Unless they happened to be sitting in the audience, in which case they would be unlikely to miss one of the most ludicrously improbable pieces of physical business ever presented on the modern stage.

We'd rehearsed it hundreds of times, first with a wastepaper bin, then with the vase itself. We could do it with our eyes closed. Every performance it had gone off without a hitch and there was no reason to suspect that tonight would be any different. I took my position stage-left, braced my left foot against the wall the way I always did and assumed the catcher's stance. The scene was unfolding with clockwork precision. The actor picked up the vase, walked two steps, tripped and lobbed it through the doorway, where I received it with my usual aplomb. And just as I did . . .

Ding-Dong.

The unmistakable sound of a doorbell rang from the speakers.

Not a vase-smash, a doorbell.

On-stage the actors froze. From Tom Baigent's booth came a seismic wave of furious muffled swearing. I carefully placed the vase on its shelf and slipped out through the back exit into the foggy chill of the darkened carpark. I quickly ran the play-by-play back through my head, desperately trying to think of some way to escape the blame. But none was forthcoming. Herb would kill me when he found me. And then Tom would bring me back to life and kill me again. On the plus side, it did get the second-biggest laugh of the night.

I remained shivering on the back step through the interval. While the audience were forming a scrum around the tea urn, those of the cast and crew who were so inclined made straight for the drinks trolley. Great crashing peals of laughter cut through the back wall, and I could only assume that they were replaying the earlier debacle.

The laughter cut louder as the door clicked open behind me. 'Here he is. Martin! What are you doing out here, you silly fucker?'

It was Graham Bickers, the most thoroughly delightful man in town, a fixture on the AmDram scene and one of the few people on the North

Island who could pull off a cravat. Graham was a straight version of Nathan Lane, and his equally spectacular wife was inside acting one of the play's most-murdered characters. Together they were perhaps the most glamorous and well-liked couple on the local non-professional theatre scene. They were friends and confidants to everyone, even the bloke who worked the secret door.

'That was fucking hilarious! Here, drink this.' Graham dropped down next to me and produced, seemingly from thin air, a flute of champagne. I'm sure he could have done it at any time, anywhere, if necessary. I might also mention that he was wearing a top hat.

'Bloke falling down a staircase three times during the will reading. A vase that turns into a doorbell. Fucking brilliant! What have you got for us in the second half?'

He had a laughing fit that lasted nearly a minute.

'You know, Graham, that was two stuff-ups too many. I don't think they'll be asking me back after this show.'

'What a load of maudlin bullshit. Course they will. Something like this always happens.'

'Not like this, surely?'

'I've been in shows where a backdrop from *South Pacific*'s come down halfway through a poignant Russian death-bed scene. Where a dog has run on stage and started barking at the main character – in this instance, a woman buried up to her waist in a mound of dirt. Where disco music has started playing during *Murder in the Cathedral*. I once saw two actors try to have a swordfight with only one sword between them. There's always going to be something. Even in your so-called proper productions.'

He clinked flutes, drained his, and refilled it from the bottle, which he also had about his person. 'I thought my wife was going to lose it up there when that vase thing happened.'

'She won't be pissed off?'

'Naah,' he assured me. 'Look, Herb Rafter'll be shat off with you for a while, and I'd steer clear of the director 'til tomorrow night, but other than that, it's just a piss-funny story to be wheeled out when the occasion demands. The broken vase story, they'll call it. It'll be remembered long after the identity of Lord William Murdersby's killer has been forgotten, I can promise you that.'

So this was what theatre people did. Turned a disaster into a funny story. A new performance piece with a life, and a run, of its own.

'All right then, I'll keep my head down in the second half.'

'You can't get out now, Martin. It's too much fucking fun.'

And with a fluttering of cape, he was gone.

Keith Delwyn called it 'the freedom to fuck up'. That was what the theatre afforded you, and that was what made it a better after-work endeavour than, say, rugby or skydiving. Here, as in the endless 'trust exercises' I saw the actors endure, there was always someone to catch you and say, 'Well, it didn't work, but good on you for trying.' You could run anything you wanted up whatever you could find for a flagpole, and if no-one saluted, it didn't really matter, because it wasn't maths; there was no right answer, and this was what gave you the freedom to fuck up.

But try explaining that to Herb Rafter.

'I don't give a flying fuck, Martin! It was a fucking shambles, not a "bold experiment that didn't quite come off"! And where does it say that you have the *freedom* to piss around with Tom's tapes? Well? I might just have to exercise my freedom to kick your fucking arse!'

This was all whispered into my face during one of the quietest scenes in the second act. I couldn't move. I was rooted to my spot behind the secret door, determined to give my three designated actions . . .

1. swinging open the secret door on cue;
2. waiting 'til someone gets shot; then
3. closing it,

. . . my full and undivided attention. Herb thundered, silently, back to his command post and Keith collapsed, woozy from the effort of not laughing out loud. He'd spent the interval mingling with the punters and informed me that 'the doorbell bit killed!'. But he did also agree that this meant not one single thing could afford to go wrong for the whole rest of the play. The secret door bit had to work smoothly, elegantly and with Swiss precision timing.

There's a scene in *You Screamed, M'Lord?* where one of the loonier guests at Murdersby Manor dresses up as Napoleon and gets shot dead in the library. Hardly unexpected and, given the performance, entirely justified. The gunman is, of course, hiding behind a secret door, a bookcase that swings slowly open, revealing a disembodied hand holding a gun. A gun that fires just one shot before receding into the darkness as the actor completes a few textbook death throes and the audience thinks 'Who? Who . . . was responsible for operating that secret door with such poise, deftness and grace?'

This scenario also requires that a gun go off, on cue, every night. The only person Herb Rafter trusted not to fuck this up was Herb Rafter. Herb had two guns, the one the audience saw and a second one, out of view, which he would fire if the first one didn't go off. Which it always did, because in spite of their reputation, prop guns almost always go off. And the chances of *two* failing to go off were so microscopic, so insanely unlikely, that there was almost no need for Herb's second back-up plan, which was for one of us to grab two large blocks of wood and smash them together. Whether this would sound as idiotic as a doorbell in place of a shattering vase was neither here nor there, because night after night, the first gun went off.

As I stood behind the hinged bookcase, braced, poised and ready for Keith Delwyn's cue, I realised that this was exactly where I wanted to be. Part of a crack team of non-professionals, all of us thinking and moving as one, unseen by the audience, but as vital to the mise en scène as the players themselves. I surveyed my crewmates. Who were these people I'd been spending every evening with for the last five weeks? What did they do during the day? Herb Rafter, the stage manager, was, in reality, in realty. Julie, his assistant, was Herb's secretary and theirs was the only workplace dynamic preserved from the real world. 'Brownie', the props master, was a milkman, and his two assistants were a dental nurse and an English professor. The lighting was supervised by an unemployed cook, and his assistant was a wealthy architect. The prompt was a very distinguished old lady, a retired music teacher with a beautiful speaking voice that was never once called upon during the entire season. But every night she'd be pacing backstage, doing her elaborate vocal warm-ups. 'Peggy Babcock,' she'd say, over and over. 'Peggy Babcock, Peggy Babcock, Peggy Babcock.' Before long everyone was saying it, and inevitably there was a 'Peggy Babcock' drinking game. You had to say it ten times quickly then take a shot. This seemed the perfect combination of two primary theatrical disciplines, diction and drunkenness.

'Prompt!' someone would cry, as the game leader stumbled on his fifteenth attempt. 'Peggy Babcock!' would come the mass shouted reply, and moments later it would be four in the morning and everyone would suddenly remember they had jobs and families to be getting back to.

And then, the next night, there we'd all be, reassembled amid the ropes and pulleys, focussed only on the play, our collective disciplines in concert with the actors on-stage, creating that wondrous illusion of life as it is lived – or would be if we were all summoned to a midnight will reading at a spooky mansion in the English countryside.

Herb was in position with the guns. Keith was mouthing the lines along with 'Napoleon'.

That champagne was fantastic. I feel great. God, I love the theatre.

Here's what happened in the next ten seconds.

Keith cued me, and stepped back onto his mark.

I swuuuung open the secret door with as much subtlety and foreboding as I could muster.

Herb raised the gun level with Napoleon's heart. His hand was gloved, as the identity – and sex – of the murderer had not yet been revealed. For the record (spoilers ahead), it was a woman.

Napoleon cried out in horror.

The audience gasped.

The gun didn't go off.

Click.

Nothing. Time stood still.

Click. Click.

Not to worry, there's always that second gun.

Click.

For the first time in theatrical history, the second gun didn't go off.

Click. Click.

Herb, his right hand still participating in the play, was unable to move. It was up to us now. At last, we would learn the answer to that age-old mystery of the stage: can two blocks of wood being smashed together possibly sound anything like a discharging pistol?

Keith turned to the two blocks.

I turned to the two blocks.

But the two blocks weren't there.

Someone had taken the two blocks of wood!

They weren't there!

On-stage Napoleon was doing exactly what you wouldn't do in real life. He was standing frozen to his spot, his face a mask of gurning terror, patiently awaiting the shot that would finish him. Eventually.

'HIT ANYTHING! HIT FUCKING ANYTHING!' whispered Herb, with ear-splitting force.

I swung round and picked up an apple box.

Keith reached over and lifted a fire extinguisher off the wall.

At exactly the same time, Brownie grabbed a chair, the elderly prompt produced a torch, and every stagehand in sight lunged for a broom, a hammer, the tea-urn – anything that would make a noise.

Napoleon braced for the shot.

I smashed the apple box to the floor, just as Keith slammed the extinguisher into the wall and, an eighth of a second later, Brownie splintered the chair into matchsticks.

Napoleon had effectively been shot three times. He reacted, grandiosely, to each impact, and then dropped to the floor like a fainting Kenneth Williams.

But even before he'd hit the deck, there came seven, eight, nine more 'gunshots'. It was too late to stop them. All over backstage, people were already mid-swing when the first shots went off. It was like the end of *Bonnie and Clyde*. Bang-bang-bang-ba-ba-bang-bang-bang. Bang. Bang.

Napoleon's body was dancing, thrashing, flailing on the ground in a hail of broken furniture. Herb struggled to adjust the trajectory of the single gun that was presumably responsible for this prolonged outburst of artillery fire and broken cups.

Bang-bang-ba-b-b-bang. Clatter. Tinkle. Bang.

Napoleon was finally dead. From exhaustion.

Which was my cue to close the secret door.

But Herb, who must have been as confused as the audience, hadn't yet withdrawn his gun-hand.

Crunch.

'FUUUCK!'

For the first time, Herb had broken either rule 2 or 3 on his list, and the audience now had to assume that the killer was a male character they hadn't yet been introduced to.

And the gun, rather than disappearing back into the darkness, dropped to the ground, where BANG! it finally discharged, its unmistakable gun-ness standing in stark contrast to the mystifying wood-chop carnival that had preceded it. The shattered Bonaparte offered one last expiratory spasm as the play's remaining characters assembled in the library and expressed bafflement as to how the victim could have been shot, despite the rather conspicuous presence of a smoking gun in the middle of the floor.

Keith and I were helpless, gone for all money. Even Herb was laughing. It was a disaster beyond any we could have imagined. And it wasn't really anybody's fault. The delirium spread across the backstage area, up into the sound booth and rained down on the blokes in lighting. Then, slowly, as everyone started to work out what had happened, the giggling began to infect the audience. Pockets of stifled hysteria were breaking out everywhere. Only the actors remained steadfast, desperate to drive the scene home and get the hell off the stage. But soon they, too, would crack.

I pressed hard against the secret door and bit down on my sleeve. I was sure my convulsions were shaking the entire set. I knew that somewhere in the crowd Graham Bickers was having an asthma attack, and that made it even funnier. Tears were rolling down my glasses. This was what it felt like, then, to have too much fucking fun.

a made bed in hell

'That's not a made bed in Hell,' I recall Mrs Dixon saying, upon inspection of my sleeping quarters at school camp one year.

That there would even be beds in Hell, let alone made ones, struck me as unlikely, but ever since that day I have striven to achieve, at the very least, the presumably minimal standard the boudoir of the underworld will require.

The first thing I noticed, as I toured the house I would be living in for the next three months, was that all the beds were made to factory showroom standards. The sheets were taut, crisp and turned back to precise and identical specifications, like it was the Sheraton, rather than suburban Takapuna on Auckland's North Shore. This may have been because Mrs Yeoman was, as she had informed me upon my arrival, an ex-nurse. One built like a brick shithouse, I might add. A brick shithouse in polyester pants, wearing Swifty Lazar's glasses.

'This is your room,' she wheezed, exhausted from the long walk down the hall. 'There are two beds, but don't get any ideas.'

None were presenting themselves, except possibly an idea for a natty hand-knitted hot-water-bottle cozy emblazoned with the flag of Canada, but I noticed immediately that Mrs Yeoman had beaten me to it.

'Are you a reader, Mr Martin?'

'Sometimes, yes.'

'There's a full set of Alistair MacLeans in the wardrobe. Feel free.'

How could I not? It was perfect. My first home away from home and it was just like home – a small bedroom in a house full of strangers.

I was eighteen and had stepped off the bus in Auckland like a wide-eyed bumpkin from Amish country. My new position as head dogsbody at an advertising agency demanded that I move north in a hurry and begin life as a boarder, with the family whose ad read the nicest. The Yeomans' featured all the usual signifiers. Their sml furn room with sep toi was in a nice hse, on a lge prop, in a pve loc, which was cls trans. What mre could you ask fr? But what really got my attention was the final line, in which no vowel had been spared: 'You won't find friendlier.' Quite a claim, and one which, initially, proved accurate.

'How much stuff have you got, Tony?'

'Two suitcases, some boxes and a stereo.'

'A stereo? We've already got a stereo.'

'Yeah, but I like to listen on headphones.'

She stared at me through those glasses, like I had just confessed to some hideous perversion.

'Well, that's a bit . . . different,' she finally blurted.

'You won't hear a thing,' I assured her.

'What kind of music, if you don't mind me asking?'

'Oh, the kind of stuff you'd see on *Radio With Pictures*,' I said, referencing the popular Sunday night rock-video parade, hosted by the cool and mysterious Karyn Hay.

'Weird stuff, you mean?'

'Not really. I'm sure I'd have at least one record you've got,' I said, with ludicrous optimism.

'We like stage musicals, mainly. Have you ever seen *Jesus Christ Superstar*?'

'Yes, I have,' I replied, as though I had enjoyed it.

'Well, I bet you haven't seen it with my husband,' she said, wagging a sausage-like digit in my face.

'Your husband? What's he . . .'

'He's in the chorus.'

'When's this?'

'They open in seven weeks. It's an amateur production, but you'd never know.'

I prayed she was right. But no.

'You'll have to come along to opening night.'

For a few moments I considered making a run for it. Bolting from the Yeomans right then and there. In retrospect, that would have been the sensible thing to do. Instead I said, 'Love to.'

Five minutes later Mrs Yeoman was – at her own insistence – carrying my cases up the stairs like some bespectacled pack mule in purple pants. I had agreed to attend my fourth amateur production of *JCS* in five years and, for the moment, I was in the landlady's good books. They would soon be rewritten.

Mr Yeoman, or Lance, as he insisted I call him, was a car-battery salesman, and so round, bearded and barefoot that I was recently surprised to learn that it was not he, but someone else entirely, who went on to make all those *Lord of the Rings* movies. He was large and welcoming and radiated the pre-eminent friendliness the advertisement had so conspicuously promised. But in all things he was subordinate to his wife, Linda, or Mrs Yeoman, as she insisted I call her.

The other resident was Lance and Linda's eight-year-old daughter, Petal, who may have been a genius or may have been something-challenged. I was never sure, as she barely said a single word during my entire time there. She mostly stayed in her room, hiding behind glasses that I could see would eventually grow to the size of her mother's. Some evenings she would join us in the sunset-flooded lounge for *The Young Doctors*, but often, apropos of nothing, she would run from the room screaming, and seconds later a bedroom door would slam shut. Then Mrs Yeoman would thunder down the hall, the door would slam again, and there would follow a muffled to-do, from which she would eventually return, exhausted, to collapse in one of the three La-Z-Boys. The tension, the discomfort, the family madness. I was home.

Mrs Yeoman never missed *The Young Doctors* and would roar with laughter throughout, as one procedural inaccuracy followed another. Lance would heap his dinner plate with leftovers and disappear downstairs to the workshop where, I soon discovered, he would sit on his own watching the same shows on a tiny black-and-white TV nestled among the many unfinished projects that cluttered his oily workbench.

The three of them seemed to circulate in three separate orbits, largely avoiding each other, except at mealtimes. Even then, their appearances would often be staggered, the meals completed in shifts. Conversations were kept to a minimum, the most spirited being those conducted by Mrs Yeoman to the television.

'Oh, that's not how you do that, you silly man!' she would scream to the oblivious Frank Spencer.

I spent most evenings in my room, with the

chunky headphones on, listening to whatever the *NME* told me to. The second bed was piled high with my albums, two crates worth, carefully freighted from home, which I played over and over on my gun-metal-grey PYE Three-In-One. It cost me $499.99 and I knew it was a good one, because when you pressed Eject on the tape deck, it took a satisfying three seconds to sliiiiide out and *thunk* open. Mmmm, nice.

After three or four evenings of this antisocial audiophilia, a loud knock cut through the four-track squall of Dunedin din, and I ripped off the headphones mid-Clean.

'Can I come in?'

The door swung open and there was Mrs Yeoman in a most unbecoming aqua tracksuit, speckled with the suggestion that a tissue had gone through the wash. As she spoke she cast a faint spotlight of disapproval across the stereo, the records and the tall stack of *Rip it Up*s. 'I was just wondering if you're all right in here,' she said, with light theatrical concern.

'Fine. Is there a problem?'

'Well, we never see you. I was beginning to think we'd done something to offend.'

'Not at all,' I insisted, politely overlooking her attire. 'I'm just a bit of a keep-to-myself type, I guess.'

'Oh, don't worry, I've seen all sorts in my time.'

It wasn't my intention to appear rude or aloof. It was just that it was my first stereo and I'd only had it for six months. For seventeen years I'd been forced to listen to Easy Listening AM Radio. The Carpenters, Gilbert O'Sullivan, Roger Whittaker and maybe, if they were feeling *really* adventurous, 'Bad Habits' by Billy Field. It was the soundtrack to someone else's life – my mother's, primarily. Finally, in 1982, I had my own set of ears and a lot of catching up to do. But Mrs Yeoman wasn't going anywhere.

'Well, I suppose it *is* time for a cup of tea,' I conceded.

'And David Attenborough's coming on,' she pointed out.

Mrs Yeoman watched David Attenborough's programmes with an A4 notepad nestled on her considerable lap. She would sometimes jot down unusual facts or statistics and the next morning would recite them to Lance over breakfast. He had been watching the same show downstairs, but would feign surprise and curiosity at every Attenborough bombshell. 'Five beaks, you say? Who would've thought?'

This particular evening, *Life on Earth* happened to be followed by a show I was interested in watching, a sketch comedy from England with the lumbering title, *Not the Nine O'Clock News*. As soon as the opening credits came on, Mrs Yeoman lunged for the enormous remote.

'Hey, this is a good show!'

'No, I'm sorry, Tony. I can't abide the language.'

She'd switched over to *Simon & Simon*, the mismatched but nicely-spoken sibling detectives. 'Last week I saw thirty seconds worth, and they used a certain word no less than three times.'

'Which word? "Thatcher"?'

'I'll write it down.' And she did. She actually wrote it down. Then, taking a deep breath, she held up the notepad. 'ARSE', it said in dispassionate capitals.

I shook my head in mock disgust. Then I excused myself, walked briskly to my room, and laughed mine off for an hour.

As long as my bed was made, Mrs Yeoman was happy. Off my own bat, I mastered her exacting style and this didn't go unnoticed.

'You can sure make a bed, Tony,' she declared one morning, as I assembled my customary Weet-Bix and brown sugar buffet.

'Thank you, Mrs Yeoman,' I replied, with forced modesty.

There followed a long silence, broken only by the sound of the boiling water, eating into the Weet-Bix like acid.

'Um . . .' She had something else to say, but was having trouble getting started.

'Yeah?' I offered.

'I couldn't help but notice the records. The covers . . . um . . .'

'Which covers?'

'Well, there's the one with the trousers . . . and the zip . . .'

She was, of course, referring to *Sticky Fingers*. But what exactly was the problem? Had I left the album's fly down? Had the popular LP exposed itself to her? 'There's no bad language or anything. What exactly is the . . .'

'It's just the whole *suggestion*, Tony.'

'What suggestion? It's an album cover.'

'There's a suggestion. You know there is.'

'But it's a very common album. Lots of people have it.'

'Well, *we* don't. And what if Petal saw it? She's only eight, you know.'

'Has she been in my room?'

'No, but you know kids.'

Not like her, I didn't.

'All right, I'll move it to the back of the pile. Behind the Dead Kennedys.'

'Tony, I haven't mentioned this up 'til now, but we are a semi-Christian household.'

'Semi?'

She winced, as though experiencing a sudden acid reflux. 'Lance isn't as . . . committed as I am,' she said, blinking rapidly behind those massive specs. 'And I don't like to impose my beliefs on others unless it's absolutely necessary.'

'Well, I don't . . . I don't know what to . . .'

'You don't have to do anything. Just keep in mind there's a certain *sensibility* here.'

'A religious sensibility?'

She winced again. 'I can't honestly say that because, well, you've heard Lance. He's not a churchgoer and he can talk a very blue streak when his mates are around. I've tried to get him to tone it down, especially for Petal's sake, but he just reminds me that I knew what I was getting into when I left Edmonton.'

'They don't have swearing in Edmonton?'

'It's a different type of person over there. Not better, I'm not saying that. Just different. But marriage is a two-way street, accepted, and like I say, I don't like to impose.'

Although, at eighteen, my moral code was still largely derived from song lyrics, I didn't feel that I had especially challenged this amorphous sensibility Mrs Yeoman was attempting to cultivate here in Takapuna. I had voiced none of my usual well-rehearsed second-hand objections to the tenets of organised religion. My language, normally streaked with its own lazy blue tinge, was kept spotless at all times. And, if I wanted to watch a TV show that was likely to contain the word 'ARSE', I would join Lance in the basement. He didn't mind a bit of 'ARSE'. He positively revelled in it.

So what exactly was she referring to? A cardboard 'suggestion' of Mick Jagger's tackle? Was this the basis of a challenge to her sensibility?

'Is there something else that's bothering you, Mrs Yeoman?'

'Well, as a matter of fact, yes.'

She plopped herself into a kitchen chair, and focussed her Hubble-like lenses on mine. 'You've been here a fortnight and you've barely made mention of your family.'

She was right. But even by the time I was eighteen my family history was so fractured, so tortuous, so painful to explain and impossible to convey without diagrams and an overhead projector that I wouldn't have inflicted it on my own worst enemy. Not that I'd need to. They'd already be in it.

'There's a reason for that,' I said. For a moment I considered following up this dramatic pronouncement with a hysterical flight to my room, Petal-style. Then the syn-drums could have come in, like at the end of *EastEnders*. But instead I came out with: 'It's just not a very interesting story.'

'I'd still like to hear it,' she said, making herself comfortable. 'Cup of tea?'

I joined her at the green Formica table and gave her the cleaned-up version. The family press-release version I had memorised for precisely such occasions. The version where the divorces are amicable and the behaviour of all parties civilised and restrained. The version where the years of bitter, acrimonious disputes, lies and manipulation are kept to a minimum. The version where nothing gets thrown and no-one gets rushed to hospital. And I kept a straight face throughout.

'Well, that's a very sad story, Tony. But I know lots

of people from broken homes and they're just like the rest of us. Except the Thompsons.'

I never did find out who the Thompsons were, as I was still considering the term 'broken homes'. I had never thought of my home, or any of my homes, as particularly 'broken'. Life went on and at least, unlike here, people talked to each other. Sure, it was often a torrent of invective filtered through a haze of paranoia, but it was conversation and it helped to pass the time.

'Thanks, Mrs Yeoman. I should be getting to work.'

'Yes. But remember, if you ever need someone to talk to, I can give you a phone number.'

'For who?'

'Father Bryant. He's very open-minded.'

'Thanks, Mrs Yeoman,' I said, leaving the room like I was heading for the bus stop. In truth, there was still ten minutes to kill. I ducked down the hall to my room, slipped between the headphones, and fired up 'Can't You Hear Me Knocking'. A priest? Fuck that. The contents of Mick Jagger's trousers would see me right for a few more years yet.

Most nights I'd come home knackered. My new job was mostly lifting and carrying or crouching in a tiny darkroom, inhaling chemicals. Every night I'd sit locked in position 2 on one of the La-Z-Boys, eating dinner off my lap and letting Ada from *The*

Young Doctors kiosk do all the talking. Then I'd stagger off to my room and listen to records until I fell asleep, dreaming about what things would be like if I was in, say, New Order, rather than Takapuna.

A harmless enough routine, I would have thought. But slowly I began to sense a certain creeping disdain from Mrs Yeoman. It was as though I wasn't merely a boarder, but a wayward teenage son, lacking motivation and drive. There was lots of 'Why don't you get out and do something?' and plenty of 'Why are you always cooped up in the dark?'. It was as if I'd never left home. Eventually, even the perfectly made bed wasn't enough.

'Tony, are you sure you're enjoying living here?'

'Very much, Mrs Yeoman. Why do you ask?'

'Well, you're not really much of a . . . participator, are you? You're always in your room.'

'I'm sorry. What activities have I been missing out on?'

'See, now, that's you being sarcastic, isn't it?'

'I'm not trying to be. I'm just not sure what you expect of me.'

'I don't expect anything.'

'Well, then – surely I'm meeting your expectations?'

'Is this how people talk at your work?'

'I'm sorry?'

'Is this how they talk in . . . advertising?'

'As far as I can tell, mostly they just say, "Hey, kid, have you stacked those crates in my car yet?"'

'Yes, well, you're on the bottom of the ladder, aren't you?'

'Yup.'

'I understand that, but it's no excuse for bad manners.'

But what exactly had I done? Or not done? I peered deep into those fat lenses, but I could see nothing that made any sense to me. This lady was dancing with herself.

I was sure my attendance at the opening night of *Jesus Christ Superstar and Three-Course Banquet* would get me back on side with Mrs Y. Certainly I dressed to impress, in my newly fashionable tweed 'bomber jacket', sharply pressed grey slacks and pointy grey shoes. As I escorted Mrs Yeoman to her seat I looked ready for a little Serious Moonlight. She was resplendent in what can only be described as an eiderdown and fanned herself with a programme, emitting hoots of recognition as, gradually, our table filled with fellow stage widows.

Ours was one of dozens of tables crammed into a theatre that, during the day, doubled as a yacht club. The walls were bedecked with boating paraphernalia: ropes and oars and Gilliganisms galore. 'Why not?' I thought. Someone's already added show tunes to the story of Our Lord, why not throw in a nautical setting? I prepared myself for the sight of Mary Magdalene making her first entrance wearing a life-jacket.

One of the three courses was a glass of Fanta and

another was a chocolate biscuit. Between them came a fabulous parmigiana, defrosted to perfection. But all this was a prelude to the steaming main course served up by one A. Lloyd Webber. *Superstar* was as I remembered it. Shithouse. Not the production itself, which was no better or worse than I had endured before. But Lloyd Webber's bilge killed with the on-side crowd, and every number brought the house down. At one point a stagehand wandered into view by mistake and he too received a round of applause. The actor playing Christ was as tough and tanned as the parmigiana, and as soon as he appeared, there was a flutter of programmes. All over the room women could be heard repeating his name. Later, in quiet bits, the men could be heard simply repeating. The second course was clearly kicking in and the fumes began to rise. I swear, during the Last Supper, I saw Jesus wafting his menu.

As for Lance Yeoman, or 'Lance Yedman' as he was listed in the programme, I couldn't see him anywhere. During the first number, I nudged Mrs Y. 'Where's Lance?'

'Can't you see him?'

The stage was a whirling tumult of rented robes and fake beards, as a dozen disciples formed a kickline of incomparable piety.

'No. Where?'

'*There*. Look.' She gestured to the contents of the largest caftan on stage. For some reason, Lance had decided to wear a fake ginger beard over the top of his real black one. A man with a beard wearing a fake beard. I defy anyone not to laugh. And despite my best efforts, laugh I did. All the way through the first half. Big mistake. Out in the foyer, at interval, the treats and the atmosphere were frosty.

'Why were you laughing, Tony?'

'The beard! You didn't find the beard funny?'

'Lance has put a lot of work into this.'

'He already has a beard . . .'

'He's taking it very seriously.'

'. . . and he's wearing another beard on top of it!'

'Oh, honestly.'

'A second beard!'

'I think it's meant to look like he's wearing a fake beard.'

'But he has a real beard.'

'Yes, but the audience are seeing the fake beard.'

'So it's intentionally fake-looking?'

'Yes.'

'But . . . it wasn't so fake that it looked like it was *meant* to look like a fake beard. If you see what I mean.'

'Well, that's what it's meant to be. A fake beard. End of story.'

Fake beard? That wasn't a fake beard in Hell. This was the craziest conversation I'd ever been involved in. Until the one on the drive home, which, foolishly, I initiated.

'Lance?'

'Yeah.'

'Can I ask you about your bear—'

Mrs Yeoman cut in like a spokesperson for Philip Morris. 'Tony, I don't think he wants to talk about . . .'

'No, what, Tony? The beard?'

'Yes. Is the beard you wear in the play meant to be your real beard or is it meant to look like a fake one?'

'Tony, don't pursue this . . .'

But Lance was genuinely stumped. 'You know, I hadn't really thought about that. I guess I just liked the beard. It's huge and red, and when you're only in the chorus, you need something like that to get noticed.'

'Of course.'

Mrs Yeoman seemed satisfied with this. 'You see, Tony? It was all part of his plan. There's a pointer for you. You should write that down.'

She leaned over and planted a fat kiss on her husband and then hummed the score of *Jesus Christ Superstar* all the way to Takapuna. My distaste could not have been more apparent had it been wearing a huge red goatee. 'How was it?' asked Petal, as we stepped through the front door, instantly doubling the number of words I'd ever heard her say.

'Your father was superb,' gushed Mrs Yeoman. 'And the whole thing was tip-top. Even Tony enjoyed himself.'

Petal had not attended the opening night, because

Lance wanted her to see the show later in the run 'when it's settled down'. I assumed by 'it' he meant the beard.

Ever since our very first conversation I had been afraid to tell Mrs Yeoman of my own interest in amateur dramatics. I failed to mention that, following my largely sterling work operating the secret door in *You Screamed, M'Lord?*, I had played 'The Amusing Constable' in a lavish mounting of Henry Fielding's 'bawdy romp', *Tom Jones*. I had hoped to secure the role of 'The Blustering Squire', but at the auditions I was roundly outblustered and had to settle for two lines at the close of Act III, one of which was 'What's all this, then?' During one matinee, a child in the front row answered this question with a loud, 'Boring and unrealistic', which was considerably more amusing than anything The Amusing Constable had to say.

It was this piffling résumé that accompanied me to Auckland, where I hoped to get a foot in with the city's biggest 'non-professional' theatre group, the New Independent.

Now, imagine for a moment that I had mentioned this to Mrs Yeoman, back when it might have been relevant to do so. Back when she first pointed out that I hadn't seen *Jesus Christ Superstar* until I'd seen it with her husband. Imagine how that would have gone down. It would have been a classic case of upstaging and she would never have forgiven me. Things would have become unbearable, instead of their present mildly uncomfortable.

But once I had successfully auditioned for the role of foppish Simon Bliss in the New Independent's December production of Noël Coward's *Hay Fever*, there was no keeping it quiet. I had seen the cattle call in the *Herald*, and the following Saturday morning I fronted up to the massive NI Theatre, which shared its looming premises with the Masons. There were about forty of us going for Simon, and my theory is that I got the part because I was the only candidate who hadn't seen the then-fashionable *Brideshead Revisited*. I was the only one who hadn't come dressed as one of the series' characters and the only one who didn't affect an impersonation of either Jeremy Irons or the other one during the audition. It was an interchangeable parade of effetely hair-swept young men clutching small volumes of poetry, with lemon-coloured sweaters flung casually round their maroon-cravated necks. They were, each and every one of them, handsome, tortured and camp. There was at least one Mr Humphries. Whereas I just did my Grytpype-Thynne voice.

'Guess what, Mrs Yeoman? I've gotten into a play, so I guess I'll be out of the house quite a lot from now on.'

'What play?'

'It's a Noël Coward thing. Just a small production.

Nothing like *Jesus Christ Superstar*.'

'What made you suddenly decide to do this?'

Now, I could have told her the truth, but how weird would it have been that I hadn't mentioned it before? So, of course, I spun some bullshit that sounded bad even before it came tumbling out. 'I guess seeing Lance do that show just . . . inspired me.'

'Really? Inspired you? So, who's it with?'

'The New Independent Theatre.'

'Right. Them. I see.'

'What?'

'Oh, nothing.'

'No, I can see it's something. What?'

'Well, it's just . . .' She removed her glasses and breathed on the lenses, which took several seconds to fog up. 'Our little group not fancy enough for you, is that it?'

'No! Of course not. I don't sing. I couldn't audition for . . . um . . .'

'*Brigadoon*.'

'Exactly! *Brigadoon*.'

'And what, may I ask, is wrong with *Brigadoon*?'

'There's singing.'

'There's also helping out backstage. Did you consider that?'

'Oh, come on, there was an ad in the paper. I can do the accent.'

'So, you're like an expert now, are you?'

'No, I'm just . . . I'm going to my room.'

Mum.

After that things went downhill, or 'Dan Hill' as I used to say, in a then-topical but still irritating reference to the singer of 'Sometimes When We Touch'. Almost overnight, Mrs Y. started to take offence at nearly everything I said and did. She would divine in even the most innocent of remarks some sort of personal affront or insult.

'Could I have some more peas, please?'

'Tony, are you suggesting I'm stingy with the peas?'

'No.'

'Good. Because I've not had any complaints yet.'

This new sensitivity would be especially apparent if I dared even refer to the rehearsals I was attending almost every night.

'I'll be late home again tonight, Mrs Yeoman.'

'Of course you will.'

'So there's no need to keep any tea out for me. I'll get something in town.'

'Fine. I'll just throw your dinner in the rubbish, will I?'

'What . . . you've already made tonight's dinner?'

'Of course not. I'll get to dinner when I'm good and ready.'

'Well, when you do, don't make any for me. That way you won't have to throw it out.'

'I'm not going to throw out perfectly good food. What do you take me for?'

Lance, who had obviously been told, said nothing. I had no allies left.

One day I came home with something so amazing that even Petal sat up and took notice. It was a 'picture-disc', an old-style 45rpm single with a picture of the band – in this case, Madness – pressed into the vinyl. Everyone gathered round, skeptical that it would even play, but the needle found the groove and within seconds 'House of Fun' was blasting from the Yeomans' rarely used speakers. Petal was so entranced by the picture-disc, and the insanely catchy song it played host to, that she would often borrow the 45 from my room and pogo round the loungeroom to its jaunty fairground paradiddle. Mrs Y. tolerated this, because 'at least she's out of her room'. But after a week of Madness, she heard on the radio that 'House of Fun' was in fact a song about going to the chemist's to buy some condoms. Now, if I hadn't realised this – and I hadn't – what were the chances that an eight-year-old had detected the contraceptive subtext in this nuttiest of number ones? The record was promptly subject to a highly localised ban.

If that wasn't the final straw, then *The Thing* certainly was. One evening Lance and Linda ventured into the city to catch a screening of *So Fine*, a long-forgotten comedy starring Ryan O'Neal as a man who starts an international craze by inventing – I'm not making this up – jeans where the arse-cheeks are cut out and replaced with see-through plastic panels. As the Yeomans' stationwagon crunched its way down the gravel drive, a truly disturbing image of Mrs Y. squeezed into a pair of these novelty pants entered my mind. I asked it to leave immediately.

Less than an hour and a half later I heard the crunching again, followed by some very loud door slams and the familiar sound of Mrs Y. struggling up the stairs, but with an urgency I'd not come across before.

'Tony! We've got a bone to pick with you.'

Fortunately she was speaking metaphorically, but this was scarcely good news. It turned out that *So Fine* had been sold out and they'd been forced to choose something else. They'd recalled me raving about a little film called *The Thing* and decided to give that a go. I was astonished. How could *So Fine* have been sold out?

Yes, I had been raving about *The Thing* but I hadn't told them to fucking go and see it! And I do recall pointing out that it was a John Carpenter splatterfest, the likes of which had, at that time, never been seen before. Rather than a zany romp with Ryan O'Neal's arseless strides, they'd copped that scene, you know the one, where Wilford Brimley literally has his hands bitten off by a dead man's chest. Then the dead bloke's head pulls itself away from his body, sprouts giant spider legs and is incinerated, screaming, by men with flame-throwers. Apparently, that doesn't happen in *Brigadoon*.

'If that's your idea of entertainment, Tony, I feel very sorry for you. Would you send your own mother along to something like that?'

There was nothing in John Carpenter's *The Thing* that my mother hadn't seen during one of her marriages, but no, I wouldn't have sent her along to it, *just as I hadn't sent the Yeomans*. But it was too late for minor details like that.

The next day when I came home from work, the house was empty, and a letter lay positioned on my pillow.

10.00am, Feb 14, 1983.

Dear Tony,
Please be informed that this is a written two weeks notice, informing you to depart our home 47 Blainey Crescent, Takapuna, by 10am Feb 28, 1983.
Sincerely,
Linda Yeoman (Mrs)

I remember little about those last two excruciating weeks. We floated through the house like ghosts, with Linda Yeoman (Mrs) refusing even to make eye-contact with me. I do recall that I continued to make my bed with rigorous precision, except on the very final morning. There were no goodbyes, as the Yeomans were all hiding in the basement. Finally, an activity they could enjoy together as a family.

With the last of my records packed into the boot, the taxi trundled away down the drive and I turned for one final look at the House of Y. I pictured Mrs Yeoman inspecting my deserted room and discovering the unmade bed, the final confirmation of all her suspicions about this insensitive young man from down south.

She'd frown, adjust her imposing bulk and wrench away the blankets to find a single crumpled sheet of A4, inscribed with the word 'ARSE', in her own ungainly hand.

And she'd never see me again. I had a new home to go to. I'd managed the impossible: I'd found friendlier.

no tarzan, mind

The name on the front door was Dowling Condos Bender. There was a Mr Condos and a Mr Bender, but oddly, no Mr Dowling. There may never have been one. Apparently, Dowling Condos Bender 'sounded fancier'. When I revisited the place twenty years later, Maureen on reception had been replaced by a younger, sleeker model and the company name had been shortened to Condos Bender. When I asked why, the new receptionist said, 'We dropped the Dowling when Mr Condos left', which I guess made sense. But when I pointed out that by retaining the Condos, she at least didn't have to answer the phone 'Bender?', she just stared at me. Maureen would have laughed.

It was 1982 and the advertisement called for a 'Junior/Artist'. Dowling Condos Bender Advertising were seeking a 'suitably qualified young person eager to enter the industry'. The candidate would need 'a keen interest in art and a driver's licence'. He or she would be working in the 'Finished Art department of Auckland's 14th largest advertising agency'. At this time I was, in fact, an eighteen-year-old forklift driver working at an army surplus store in Hamilton, a city now known as the 'suicide capital of New Zealand'. (The locals aren't happy about this, by the way, but my mother, still a resident, has seen the silver lining. 'At last, something we're good at,' she says. 'Take that, Dunedin!' She has even suggested an electronic sign at the city limit, trumpeting the catchphrase and ticking over whenever unhappy citizens top themselves.) My battered manila pocket contained the usual sixth form art department cliches, but miraculously, mine was the name pulled out of the, no doubt very stylish, hat.

After Hamilton, Auckland was like New York. The ad agency was impossibly glamorous compared with the army surplus store, where I had spent much of my time telling men in camouflage jackets and mirrored sunglasses, 'No, we don't have any larger knives.' Here, people were urbane and creative, and there were no porno tapes screened in the lunchroom or employees forced into a canvas sack, beaten, hoisted to the ceiling on their own forklift and left there all afternoon.

The DCB Finished Art department occupied the

first floor of a compact eight-storey circular building, which was the very height of architectural fashion in this, the year Ultravox went to number one with 'Vienna'. The offices splayed out from a central column, wagon wheel-style, and in each there beavered an artist or typographer, someone composing a magazine advertisement or storyboarding a TV commercial. All done by hand in this, a time before computers – Ultravox may have had one, but there were none at Dowling Condos Bender. The work was intricate and the processes mysterious, combining a number of arcane crafts from the darkroom to the drawing board. My job, however, was loading crates of piss into the boots of people's cars.

For this is what the junior did. Oh, there were a few hours working in the darkroom, and the odd bit of filing and courier work, but mostly it was loading piss into the boot. First, I would take the orders. This could take an afternoon, wandering from office to office, writing down who wanted what. Some wanted ten or twenty crates. Then I would phone in the order, and two hours later an eighteen-wheel supertanker would pull up and dump it all on the kerb. A mountain of alcohol, soon to be conquered. These agency types were sinking a power of piss, and I was carrying it down to their cars, while upstairs award-winning print campaigns were being spun from thin air. By drunks.

One day I approached the production manager, a man whose boot and, consequently, belt were groaning with beer. A man whose mammoth gut forced one to speculate that his genitals could only be seen via a series of 7-Eleven-style security mirrors. A man who could be interrupted spilling an egg sandwich down the front of his shirt at any time of the day or night. A man who hated me.

'Mr Blore, about my job description.'

'Yeah, what about it?'

'Well, I seem to spend most of my time stacking crates of beer.'

'So?'

'The ad said you wanted a junior artist.'

'Then stack them more artistically.'

Mr Blore went on to point out that the ad had actually read 'Junior/Artist', meaning a Junior *and* an Artist. And that the piss-stacking part fell under the Junior side of the equation and that, as far as he was concerned, was the entire equation. 'I wanted a Junior, that's all. It was bloody Creative who added "Artist" in case we later needed someone who could be hands-on in the department.'

Which, for my information, young man, they didn't, don't and probably won't. Mr Blore rummaged about in his roomy slacks, fished out his car keys, and slung them across the room. 'Don't forget to leave me a couple of roadies on the passenger seat.'

So that was how I got the job. All they needed was a shitkicker. And if I really was someone with an eye for type, wouldn't I have spotted that slash between 'Junior' and 'Artist'? There was, however, in the dazzling new vernacular of 1982, an 'upside'. Providing the piss was stacked and the lunches delivered, I was free to mingle in the department and assist the art directors with minor typographical tasks. And I could work at night if I wanted, for no extra pay, and use that time to learn what I was assured were 'the ropes'. I was trained in the use of the bromide camera, a massive now-extinct system of lenses and handles and chemical baths, which could, after several minutes, enlarge or reduce a piece of type up to 100 per cent in either direction, the end result being like a razor-sharp photocopy. These copies would then be sliced up with a scalpel, waxed, and pasted onto a large piece of cardboard to create the master artwork for, say, a newspaper advertisement for 'an insane never-to-be-repeated offer'. Sometimes they'd ask me to make a letter 'B' two per cent larger. Or reduce a comma by half. One time I was asked to make an ampersand look 'less like a penis'. And after spending hundreds of hours in that tiny wedge-shaped darkroom, hunched over the bromide camera, inhaling chemicals, I started to work it all out.

It seemed the tools of this trade were the very letters of the alphabet, twisted and compacted into seductive logos, urgent messages and tart little sentences that dolloped onto every magazine ad, and floated through every TV commercial and across every billboard and T-shirt and cigarette packet and sock in the land. And these pithy, hysterical, burnished swathes of type were hand-made, hand-photographed, hand-waxed, hand-trimmed and hand-positioned in a procession of procedures that could now easily be achieved by any nine-year-old with PhotoShop. Turns out I was coming in at the arse-end of something that, in a few short years, would be extinct: finished art by hand.

I had one advantage. The only subject I'd excelled in at school, and in fact, only one small part of that subject, was Technical Drawing. Not the actual technical drawing part, at which I was, in the words of Mr Oorloff, 'shit-tacular'. No, the part where you had to write neatly under the drawings in tiny, precise lettering, like the kind you'd find in a serial killer's notebook. That, I could do. And there were other factors. I hand-drew all the titles for the school 'video news'. The headings for my essays were always far better than what followed. And I was a Letraset fetishist. Was this meagre bag of twigs enough to get me in the door at the Dowling Condos Bender Finished Art department? Perhaps I was just a foppish young dilettante from down south, fiddling about with the grown-ups' stuff, occasionally reducing or enlarging it, but essentially contributing nothing. Part of my job at the army surplus store had been ticket-writing, and I had a garish hand-drawn example of this on my office wall. The phrase, 'You've never seen bayonets at prices like these!!!' was inelegantly conceived, but elaborately rendered. Over at the knife counter I was 'quite the Andy Fuckin' Warhol'. But here among actual typographic artists, I realised I was truly mucking around down the shallow end. For starters, my tickets were not written in any known fonts. There was clearly no quota on exclamation marks!!! And often, in the middle of a word, the letters would start to crowd togetherasIranoutofspace, something you rarely saw in published commercial art. My folio exhibits were slightly more professional examples of the kind of thing you might tattoo on your ring-binder during Geography.

But I could see what they were getting at here. It was something about the way the letters went together, that was what this game was all about. And you could tell that some were good at it and others weren't. But I was neither. I was sitting in the corner, wearing a triangular hat. I needed someone in the department to put their hand up, to mentor me and guide me through the lettery thickets. But no-one had time for that. Lettery thickets? What the fuck are you talking about? And isn't that the piss truck?

The new senior art director was Jock Mahoney, a tightly wound man in his mid-thirties with a face so red it seemed an explosion must surely be imminent. His moustache looked like it wanted to take you down to the station for questioning. His hair was unusual, to say the least, but his carefully maintained eyeline seemed to imply, 'Don't look up there. There's nothing to see.' He was jet-lagged and had the slightly wary air of someone who is slowly adjusting to a world where everyone finds their accent hilarious. To my ear, he sounded Scottish. And these were the first words he ever said to me: 'Jock Mahoney. No Tarzan, mind.'

And then he smiled, as if he knew it would make no sense to me. But I understood immediately. What he meant was: 'My name is Jock Mahoney. Not the identically named actor who briefly and unmemorably played Tarzan back in the early sixties, mind you.'

What an insane way to introduce yourself. This bloke would have to be watched. His handshake was firm but fair. 'What've they got you doing?' he enquired.

'I'm the junior-slash-artist.'

'Oh, yeah? Let me show you something.'

Jock dumped his elaborate-but-manly leather bag on an ergonomic chair and slid a large piece of cartridge paper onto the drawing board. From nowhere he produced a stick of charcoal and with a few quick, impressive strokes, executed a large number '1' in what appeared to be perfect Helvetica.

'Know what that is?' he asked.

'What?'

'That's how many sugars I take.' Then he exploded into laughter, like it was the funniest joke since . . . well, since that one about Tarzan. 'Sorry . . . just taking the piss,' he managed through the tears. Regaining his composure, he climbed aboard an office chair that was set far too high for him. Unable to find the lever, which had broken off, he attempted to rotate nonchalantly with his tip-toes.

'You think I'm Scottish, don't you?'

'Um . . . are you not?'

'I'm a Geordie. Know what a Geordie is?'

'You're . . . from Jordan?' I really had no idea.

'Newcastle!' he hissed.

To me, Newcastle was a place in Australia made famous by a popular novelty song of the seventies, which repeatedly advised the listener to 'never let a chance go by'.

'On Tyne?' he added, as though it would clear everything up.

'I'm sorry, I . . . I don't understand what you're saying,' I stammered.

'*I'm not from fuckin' Scotland!*' he insisted, forgetting that I had never said he was. I stared at him, trying desperately not to look at the top of his head.

He changed tack. 'Have you seen my folio?'

Was it missing? I began to look around.

For the Geordie, this was the final straw. 'Oh, we're not communicating on any fuckin' level, are we?'

It was hard to argue. Between the folio I hadn't

seen, the on-Tyne thing and the reference to a very obscure namesake who once played Tarzan, he was right. There was no communication here. This guy was nuts. 'I'm sorry, Mr Mahoney, I'm going to have to pull the plug on this. Can we —'

Suddenly he was on his feet. 'Let's get some lunch. Just you and me.'

It would have seemed an unusual suggestion for 10am, had this not been the world of advertising. Here 'lunch' was its own unit of time, equivalent to about six-and-a-half earth-hours and falling anywhere between 9.30 and six in the evening. But could I allow myself to leave the building with this, what was he again . . . Geordie?

'Look, I don't know, I've got . . . um . . .' I didn't want to tell him about the piss-ordering system until I had to. He looked like he'd be up for about sixteen crates right there and then.

'Tiny, tiny balls? Is that what you've got, Mr Martin, Barton & Fargo?' he said, referencing a famous joke from the then-popular *Benny Hill Show*. I was impressed by the way he didn't stretch the Fargo, as an amateur would have, and, not wanting to perpetuate the tiny balls thing, agreed to go to lunch at 10.04.

The Geordie had been in our country for less than twenty-four hours, and already the rear-view mirror of his pristine rental car was adorned with football memorabilia. But as I knew sweet bugger-all about sport, this was not proving to be the conversation-starter he had hoped for.

'You're not into the football?'

'No.'

As he flitted impatiently from lane to lane down Symonds Street at its busiest, I wondered whether they drove on the same side of the road in this Newcastle of which he spoke. Alarmingly, he would change lanes while keeping one eye on me, which I assumed was to prevent me stealing a glance at his 'hair'.

'You look like you could do with a feed.'

'Sure. Where are we going, Geordie?'

I took his genuine amusement at this to be an all-clear to keep calling him it.

'I thought we'd go back to my hotel.'

Before I could wrench open the door and fling myself from the moving vehicle, he explained that the wine bar at the Excelsior stocked some obscure pommy beer that made him feel at home. It was now 10.09. It appeared that today we would be 'starting early'.

'Fuckin' balls on this guy!' said Jock, through a gritted moustache. An enormous Maori dude was walking coolly across the street in front of us, forcing the Geordie to slow down. As we cruised past the cheerfully oblivious giant, Jock rolled down his window and declared with extravagant theatrical sarcasm, 'Oh, yes! Cars bounce off me!'

And then he tore off, giggling like a girl. The Maori was given no opportunity to reply and the two never spoke again.

'Like that one?' beamed the Geordie.

'Sure,' I said.

Jock had a million of them, and over the next twelve months I would hear them all.

The wine bar at the Excelsior was velvet-lined and dandyish. It felt as though Peter Wyngarde might walk in at any moment and order something absurd. The light was flattering and the nuts were complimentary. But it was not somewhere to be at that time of the morning. I hadn't had any breakfast and here I was necking a jet-black Marmite-flavoured beer from o'er the faraway Tyne.

'You like it, Fargo?'

So it was Fargo now, was it?

'To be honest, it's a bit early in the day for me.'

'For you it is, but for me it's still last night.'

For a moment I imagined that Jock Mahoney was going to remain on Geordie time forever, as if this would somehow force the entire country to adjust to his way of doing things. Then he admitted that he didn't officially start 'til next Monday, and that he'd just popped in that morning to feel everyone out. Having not been felt out for some time, I decided not to ask why the shitkicker had been singled out for the Excelsior treatment. Jock explained anyway. It seemed his wife and kids wouldn't be arriving for another week, and he'd taken an instant dislike to the creative director because he was 'from London'. He needed an 'inside man', someone who could take him through the DCB players from an objective standpoint. Who were the good guys and who were the, as he put it, 'twats'? He intended to hit the ground running on Monday, and he wanted to know everyone's strengths and weaknesses in advance. Half an hour earlier I had been removing a dead rat from the ladies toilets; now I was being offered the role of consigliore to the new senior art director. I skolled the last of the foul Geordie potion and ordered a glass of white wine.

'You a poofter, Fargo?'

'What?'

'White fuckin' wine? Where's your girl's bike?'

'We're in a wine bar.'

'I'm just saying.'

'Saying what?'

'A cheeky chardonnay . . . no interest in football . . .'

'So therefore I'm . . . taking it up the arse?'

'Steady on!'

My drink arrived and the sparkling banter abated.

'Tell me about Bevans.'

Bevans whisky was one of DCB's most prestigious clients. The Geordie and two other art directors would be pitching ideas for the new Bevans magazine campaign next week. He wanted me to provide him with a form guide. The wine arrived and suddenly he couldn't shut me up.

'Well, Brett and Lydia will probably do something twenties art deco, you know, kind of Jeeves and Woosterish, while, knowing Victor and Malcolm, it'll be a blank page with the bottle in the bottom right-hand corner and a single word in the centre.'

'What sort of word?'

'Oh, you know . . . "Splendid" . . . "Enchanting" or maybe . . . "Incomparable".'

'With an exclamation mark?' The Geordie was loving it.

'Undoubtedly!' I said. So this was what it was like, trading badinage with a peer, exchanging bon mots with a contemporary, across the bar of a plush industry haunt. Why, isn't that Tristan from O&M, lunching with an A&R from K&B?

'So, are you pitching?' he asked.

'No, no. I'm not . . . they don't . . .' The illusion had lasted all of twenty-five seconds.

'Why not? You should do one. What's their catchphrase?'

'He forgot the Bevans.' I had bromided those words over a hundred times.

'That and a picture, that's all you need. Have a crack. I'm off to bed.' And with that he polished off his third schooner of Newcastle cough syrup and disappeared upstairs, leaving me to make my own way back to work on, presumably, my girl's bike.

★

The Geordie's winning submission for the new Bevans campaign depicted an enormous luxury ocean liner steaming out of port, while a single tuxedoed gentleman paddled elegantly back to shore because, as the type explained, 'He forgot the Bevans'. My badly received effort used the famous shot from *The French Connection* where Gene Hackman graphically guns down a hired goon at the end of the celebrated car chase because, as the type explained, 'He forgot the Bevans'. Jock smiled when he saw it, but it was a smile of disappointment. He handed it back to me and said that no-one got anywhere in this game by being a smartarse. This from the newly crowned biggest smartarse in the art department. But, despite what he thought, I was serious about my idea. I really thought we could get the rights to that shot and it would make for a funny ad. My inability to see why we couldn't and why it wouldn't explains why, in the long-term, I would have no future in advertising.

'Besides,' he added. 'Your kerning's shite.'

'My what?'

'Do you not say "kerning" here?'

Apparently we did, but I hadn't been paying attention. Jock snatched back my artwork and slapped it on the drawing board, securing it with a strip of masking tape. Then he swung down a large magnifying glass with a light in it and subjected my hand-rendered 'He forgot the Bevans' to much closer scrutiny than it had been designed to withstand.

'Look at your "Bevans". You've done the face okay – traced it, I'm guessing – but what's with the gap?'

'What gap?'

'Between the "B" and the "e".'

'It's correct.'

'Correct mathematically, but not correct to the eye.'

'How's that?'

'Capital "B", small "e", they curve away from each other. You need to snuggle the arse of the "e" into the belly of the "B" a bit. See?'

He was right. It looked much better snuggled. 'Then, because there's what we call negative space under the wing of the "v", you could, if you wanted, wedge the left hand of the "v" back into the nose of the "e".'

Of course you could.

'But not too much. Same goes for the "v" into the "a", although there's less negative space there, so there's no need to wedge. The "a" and the "n", they're back to back, so keep them loose, but not tight-loose. There's no apostrophe after the "n", so you might want to curl the tail of your "s" back there a smidge. Or not. That's your kerning.'

'Kerning'. See how the arse of the 'e' needs to back up into the mouth of the 'K' a bit? For it to be correct to the eye. That's your kerning, right there.

And mine was shite. Except for the 'f' and the 'o' in 'forgot'. There, 'probably by accident', I'd allowed the first 'o' to nuzzle under the shoulder of the 'f'. That solitary example was the only one even close to acceptable or, as the Geordie mystifyingly put it: 'Good enough for pit-work.'

'The idea is to get all the letters working as a team,' he explained. 'You've got them standing round like awkward debutantes at a school formal.'

It was a matter of tiny increments. Not enough kerning and you had a sentence full of wallflowers; too much, and suddenly your 'w' was 'all hands'.

Every moment in which I wasn't lugging the contents of Liquorland or emasculating ampersands, he had me writing out the alphabet in black felt pen on ream after ream of drawing paper. Over the next year I was to become quite proficient at that writing you see slashed across advertisements, where it appears that someone has hastily-but-elegantly scrawled 'Hurry last days!!!' on an existing piece of artwork. I suggested that 'Hurry last days!!!' would be an amusing phrase to have seen graffitied on a wall in ancient Pompeii. The Geordie made me write it a thousand more times, which was fair. I worked out that the key to cracking it was the lower case 'a'. You can always spot a typographer, because even on a shopping list they'll write it like this: 'a'. Whereas a normal person will write it like this: 'ɑ'. Once I had mastered the 'a', I was ready to take a slash on any ad the Geordie wanted. A full-page newspaper ad for Drench 'n' Go cattle drench once featured my casually tossed-off 'Now protects against the bloat!' It received glowing notices and I was invited to join the art directors at a lunch which lasted well into the next week.

All the sheets of Letraset which had been depleted of useful letters were mine to practise with. I learnt to kern using words primarily composed of Xs, Zs, and Qs.

'That's shithouse,' said the Geordie, having discovered a new word and relishing any opportunity to deploy it. He was referring to my dummy magazine campaign for XXXQZ vodka. 'You're over-kerning.'

'I'm what?'

'Your words look like fuckin' accordions!'

'That could be because of all the Xs.'

'No, no, look; you're trying too hard. They're all over each other.'

As the magnifying glass swung down, I could feel a lovemaking metaphor coming on and the Geordie didn't disappoint, with a deliciously fruity analysis of the type before him. He spoke of letters tickling and frotting and goosing each other. The tail of a 'g' could grope the neck of the 'd' below it or a large 'X' might straddle a small 'o'. I once recall the marketing manager of Teleco TV Rentals being startled by Jock describing the 'T' in 'TV' as 'fisting' the 'O' in 'Teleco'. I wondered if maybe Jock wasn't getting any at home.

'All these lines need loosening up. You've got to massage the words. Use the negative space. Find the music.'

I knew I could do it. I just needed some vowels.

Once you knew what bad kerning looked like, you'd start to see it everywhere. The Geordie and I would spend the lunch hour wandering K. Road looking for typographic misdemeanours, taking particular delight in The Shop Where The Owner Has Tried To Do His Own Sign. Jock's favourite was PHILIP ANG Electrical, where bad spacing created the impression that the shop was called PHIL IPANG Electrical. For weeks we bombarded the tiny store with calls, demanding to speak to 'Mr Ipang', until eventually the kerning was corrected.

Between typographic vendettas and attempting to 'find the music', I received daily tutorials on the latter history of Newcastle-on-Tyne. A relentlessly grim upbringing had seen the young Jock Mahoney pursued by street gangs and beaten because of his artistic demeanour and ever-present easel, which also slowed his escape. In this battleship-greyest of burgs, the unemployed supposedly outnumbered the working by four to one. Jock had taped a huge black-and-white photograph of the Newcastle marathon to the wall of his office. In it, 20 000 locals in tracksuits could be seen streaming out of the city. Across the bottom he had added a caption: 'Job advertised in London'. No-one else knew what the fuck he was on about, but for me he was both an exhausting and a compelling figure. And an infuriating one. He would often respond to things I would say by screaming, 'Y'askin' me or tellin' me?' This was because I shared, with many of my countrymen, a tendency to 'go up' at the end of sentences. Thus, 'I'm going down the shops,' becomes 'I'm going down the shops?' Often this sentence would be appended with an inexplicable 'Eh?' It's a Kiwi thing. Everybody does it. But would the fucking Geordie ever let it rest?

'I'm off to pick up that typesetting.'

'Y'askin' me or tellin' me?'

'The new transparencies have arrived.'

'Y'askin' me or tellin' me?'

'It's the fire alarm! We've got to get out of here!'

'Y'askin' me or tellin' me?'

'You're an asshole, Jock.'

'Y'askin' me or tellin' me?'

I think the moment I finally won him over came during one of his many lectures on the dangers of over-kerning. He was telling me how, in the seventies, someone had designed a cover for a reprint of the children's classic 'MY FRIEND FLICKA'. Unfortunately, they had kerned the 'L' and the 'I' in 'FLICKA' too close, so that when the cover was reduced in newspaper ads it appeared to read 'MY FRIEND FUCKA'. This problem occurred whenever the word 'FLICK' was spelt with capital letters, and had become known in the trade as 'My Friend

Fucka Syndrome'. I replied that I had seen a similar thing happen on television, during credits for films starring 'CLINT EASTWOOD'. Jock was so impressed with that one he actually wrote it down. Beautifully.

One day a stomach entered my office, followed moments later by its owner-operator, Mr Blore. He sat down, and when the undulations had subsided, proceeded to tell me that the Geordie had gone to Chicago for a week. He couldn't tell me why, but there followed an elaborate series of winks and nudges, a possibly alcohol-fuelled pantomime, which seemed to suggest that Jock's week off had something to do with his hair.

And he wasn't wrong.

When Jock returned, his hair had been somehow reconfigured into individual sprigs, planted equidistantly in a grid formation. It was a tiny cornfield of deceit. And to make matters worse, a tiny bleeding cornfield.

'It's just the first instalment,' he insisted, producing photographs of a footballer who was much further down the hair transplant track, to the point where he was now regularly going down waterslides.

The Geordie and I had never actually talked about his hair before, so I was uncertain how to proceed. Frankly, it looked like he had been dragged behind a horse through a bed of nails, but I thought it best not to mention this.

'Have you thought about a hat?' I offered.

'Can't disturb the pitch.'

'How many instalments?'

'Three more this year.'

'Why Chicago?'

'They're at the forefront of strand-by-strand.'

'I can see that.'

Now that the hair was out in the open, the Geordie seemed to calm down a bit, and there was less 'Y'askin' me or tellin' me?' But others in the firm were less kind about the transplant and the jokes quickly snowballed. The final indignity came when he fell asleep at his board one day, and Mr Blore went to work with some of the plastic figurines from a promotional Drench 'n' Go diorama. Jock awoke to discover a tiny tractor and three cows nestled between the rows of corn.

Whether these minor cruelties contributed to the Geordie's decision to accept a job at Perrett Twentyman Giles, I cannot say. He dropped this bombshell one Tuesday afternoon outside Ipang Electrical, but said that it wasn't goodbye as PTG was right next door to DCB. Then, to cheer me up, he immediately performed the entire 'Book Club' sketch from George Carlin's *A Place For My Stuff!* album. Apparently, he'd spent weeks memorising it. Neither I, the two passers-by, nor a man I took to be Phil Ipang himself had ever heard the piece performed in a Geordie accent, and the effect was hypnotic. But I couldn't help feeling that the gesture was both inappropriate and a bit sad.

'Is it more money, is that it?'
'We'll still see each other,' he said.
'Yeah?'
'Yeah,' he insisted.
'Y'askin' me or tellin' me?'

We only bumped into each other one time after that. It was an awkward encounter at the sandwich shop. He had with him a young man I recognised as the PTG junior. I think I overheard the Geordie explaining how the "N" on the 'Four 'N Twenty' logo ought to be smaller, but when they saw me, he clammed right up. We had a perfectly pleasant, but somewhat forced, conversation. Then I think he started going to a different sandwich shop. Soon after, I left the agency and the world of typography altogether. I later heard that Jock had left New Zealand and returned to a land where beer can be eaten with a spoon and artists' easels are administered anally.

After that I kind of forgot about the Geordie until many, many years later when very late one night, on cable TV, they ran one of the Jock Mahoney Tarzan movies. As the opening credits rolled and I saw that long-forgotten name, I couldn't help but notice that the kerning was shite.

the yeti

Ponsonby Road at 6:30 in the morning is not the sort of place you'd expect to find a bald German in a dressing gown, leaning out of his car, offering you some hot stew. 'Dorny. You vant zum hort schtoo?'

Gunter was my new landlord and 'Dorny' was Gunter's way of saying my first name.

'You vant zum hort schtoo do dake do verk, Dorny? I gort chew a Thermoosh vool.' He waved the tartan Thermos wildly, all the time keeping pace with me in his shuddering Mk III Zephyr, as I trudged to work in the dark. 'Da Meesus made doo blardy marcha da ztoof. Ve gorda shurploosh!'

'A surplus of stew?'

'You gorda dake zum of deese schtoo, Dorny.'

'I don't need any stew, thanks, Gunter. No offence.' With the ten bucks I saved every week by getting up at six and walking all the way to work in the city, I could now afford to buy my own damn schtoo.

'Id's goot schtoo. You rheally missink out 'ere.'

Gunter Baumann was a nuggetty, gnomelike, Swiss–German immigrant who resembled a more robust version of Little Jackie Wright, that tiny unfortunate who used to get slapped about the head, week-in, week-out, on *The Benny Hill Show*. Little Jackie Wright passed away a few years ago. Massive head injuries, the coroner said. Gunter looked like Little Jackie Wright after a can of Popeye's magic spinach. That he would chase you up the street in his car at 6:30 in the morning just to furnish you with a Thermos full of hot stew was typical of his warm, if lunatic, hospitality.

'I'll see you tonight, Gunter. Thanks again.'

'Zeeya vor dee, Dorny. Ve're hafink schtoo!' And off he chugged in the grey primer-painted Mk III, hunched over the wheel, his stripey mental-home pyjamas buttoned to the neck.

Gunter and Violet's three-guest boarding house, a crumbling conglomeration of weatherboards held together by kak-brown paint, lay at the bottom of a hill near the Ponsonby–Grey Lynn border. The neighbours were either enormous Pacific Islanders or emaciated vegan students; it didn't matter which, every house had a stereo blaring 'Buffalo Soldier' into the street and a car up on blocks in the front yard. According to the district's only Swiss–German, the locals fitted into one of two categories: 'broots' (brutes) or 'crunks' (cranks).

'Whole lotta blardy broots out da froont doday, Dorny, magin' like zilly boogers. And zum blardy crunk's lefta pile orf orld blardy ironink borts 'n' zhit out orn da nature-strib. Bodados?'

'I'll have some potatoes, sure. Thanks, Gunter.'

'Yuh loog lighe ya neet zum upholschtery orn dem schkeeny bones orf yorsch.'

He heaped a splattering of mash onto my already overloaded plate. It was just Gunter and me for tea as Violet, his large but fragile Samoan bride of over twenty years, was exhausted from the effort of producing the aforementioned shurploosh. She'd set the table and gone to bed. The other two residents, 'Gherant' (Grant) and 'Pieter' (Pieter), were out for the evening, leaving mein host and me with enough stew to unleash a fucking stewnami on all the broots and crunks making like zilly boogers out da froont.

'Look! Dere day go again, dose blardy mon-keese!'

I raced to the kitchen window in time to see two small girls on tricycles squeaking harmlessly past the letterbox. 'It's just some kids, Gunter. You're getting worked up again.'

'Aw, crarms!' (crumbs) he said, collapsing onto a tiny stool, dabbing at his forehead with a folded hankie. 'Zorry, Dorny, I'm orl blardy frarn-tic, vort vif da meesus orl crook 'n' dat.'

Gunter and Violet were both in a state of graceful decline, at an age where getting out of a chair required careful planning. 'I'm delling you, Dorny. Ven you gedd do shixty-fife, id's *schink* or blardy *schvim*!'

There were no children, only the many boarders – all men – who came and went, each of whom soon learnt not to underestimate the wiles and surveillance abilities of our seemingly decrepit hosts. Violet had only one rule: 'No with the monkey business', or, as Gunter put it: 'No vid da farny boogers'. Which meant sex. 'No with the sex.'

Which, it is tragic to report, didn't affect me in the slightest, as the only one of us lucky enough to have someone with whom to conduct any monkey business was Pieter. And for Pieter Malkmus, a slick James Woods-like Dutchman I'd been through high school with back in Hamilton, business was good.

'I can hear monkey business!' Violet would shout, belting the wall of her bedroom with an empty bedpan.

'Farny boogers!' Gunter would add, before embarking on a coughing fit that lasted until dawn.

Pieter was an immensely likeable gadabout, a man who could talk you into paying his week's rent – 'Der schpondoolie' as Gunter called it – and make it seem like he was doing you a favour. Women fell for his bullshit big-time, and I was kept awake nightly by his metronomic exertions with Claudia, an apparently inexhaustible girlfriend who was stunningly beautiful and kept excellent time. With their relentless picture-rattling drumbeat on one side and the accusatory bedpan clanging at the other, it was like trying to sleep in a munitions factory. 'Oh, yes! Oh, FUCK, yes! Oh, YES!'

'Hey! You kids! Enough with the monkey business!'

'Ohh! Ohh! Ohh! Ohh!'

'Cudditout, ya blardy broots!'

'OHH, YESSSSS!'

CLANG! CLANG! CLANG! CLANG! CLANG!

And then my alarm would go off and it would be time to get up and go to work.

'Ohh! Ohh! Ohh!'

'Oh, nord *again*, ya blardy mon-keese!'

I could still hear them while I was under the shower.

'Tony, you're a good boy, no monkey business from you.'

'Thanks for pointing that out, Mrs B.'

Violet wasn't a big fan of Pieter, but she did like me and the third boarder, Grant, a hulking meteorologist who was in training for a six-month stint at an Antarctic weather station. Grant had charged me with a special responsibility: if, while he was away, a new U2 album were to be released, I was to get a copy down to the South Pole as soon as possible. I said that, if I could, I'd get *every* copy down there, but Grant wasn't amused. U2 was like a religion to him, and with his room being way down the back, he could worship at full volume.

'Dat Gherant's a goot one, init?'

'Yeah, he's good.'

'Peace?'

'I'm good for peas, thanks.'

'He votches der nyoos, ya know.'

'The news?'

'E's da ornly blardy one off yas dats effa votched da nyoos.'

In Gunter's view, watching the news was a sign that you were taking life seriously. 'Da rescht orf yas joozt votchin' dose blardy Ronnees.'

He was referring to *The Two Ronnies*, but 'dose blardy Ronnees' meant pretty much anything that wasn't the news, the only show Gunter himself watched with any regularity. Although some nights he would stand in the doorway of the TV room, polishing his noggin with one hand and attempting to follow the storyline of Violet's favourite programme 'Da Soolimins' (*The Sullivans*). But if you caught him doing this, he'd suddenly swivel round, flailing his hand, as though swatting at an invisible moth.

'Da Soolimins, Dose Ronnees, Da Hazzart Blardy Dooks, itch orl blardy roobish,' he'd rail. 'Der nyoos, dats vere you shee vots blardy goin' orn in da *real* vorlt. Lighe blardy dornadoes an schnakes an hagzidends an zhit.'

Tornadoes and snakes and accidents and shit. That

was what was going on in the real world. Stew and monkey business and ironing boards on the nature-strip. That was what was going on in Gunter's.

Gunter, in keeping with his wife's decree, espoused a 'no farny boogers' doctrine when she was around, but when she wasn't he seemed to derive vicarious pleasure from Pieter's antics. Pieter would hold court at the breakfast table describing, in embarrassing detail, his and Claudia's latest bedroom experiments, while Gunter would potter about, adjusting his knick-knacks and listening in. As Pieter piled outrage upon outrage, Gunter would blush and fan himself with a magazine, like a Southern belle. 'Crarms!' he'd say, or 'Oh, gorsh!' Pieter lived for these responses and would refuse to stop until he'd elicited at least one of each.

'Last night we did it in a church,' he once announced.

'What church?' I enquired.

'Just up the road.'

'Crarms!'

'What? Just up here?' Grant wasn't buying it.

'Standing up, at the back. No-one even knew what we were doing.'

'Oh, gorsh!'

But Gunter had a good nose for the fanciful, and if he suspected you were pulling his leg he'd bark out this abrupt verdict: 'Torknaloadasheet!'

'It's true. I'm telling you.'

'Nah nah nah,' he'd wave, wandering off in disgust. 'Loadasheet. Marks me blardy seek.'

One morning, Pieter piqued Gunter's interest with a strange request. 'Gunter, can I have the empty Marmite jar?'

'Vod? Vodger von dat vor?'

Pieter proceeded to tell Gunter of a then-widespread rumour concerning a certain local television personality. The gentleman concerned had supposedly been admitted to hospital in the early hours of the morning with, as the teller of the story always put it, 'a Marmite jar up his arse'. Rumour also had it that the beloved entertainer was part-owner of a small pottery shop located in our very suburb. Regardless of whether any of this was true, the story had given rise to an amusing local custom. The idea was that whenever you finished a jar of Marmite, you'd hide the empty vessel in your pocket, and deposit it somewhere amongst the exhibits at the poor bloke's pottery shop. A sort of reverse-shoplifting exercise. Often you'd walk past and see five or six empty jars, carefully scattered among the vases and teapots, little time bombs awaiting discovery by the fuming proprietor. Pieter had observed that our jar of Marmite, an anus-stretching extra large family size specimen, had finally run dry, and he was determined that we make our contribution to this popular neighbourhood ritual.

'Torknaloadasheet!'

'That's what they say. Apparently, it took five hours to extricate.'

'Oh, my God,' said Grant. 'It's glass! Imagine if it broke!'

Everyone screamed at the thought, except Gunter, who said, 'Crarms!'

'Have you noticed he hosts that show standing up now?' added Grant.

'Ohh, yer *torknaloadasheet*! Dat bloke vooden be puddin dem jarse up dere. Duddin maig zense.'

'Well, can I have the jar anyway? I think this is something we have to do.'

'No, ya blardy karnt! You shick en da blardy hett, chew are.'

Gunter promptly lay the jar down in the sink, covered it with a teatowel and smashed it with a hammer. 'Now, garn do zum blardy verk, ya blardy vo-begonse!'

It was the first time any of us had been called 'woebegones'. But that wasn't what we were thinking. What we were thinking was: where the fuck did that hammer suddenly come from?

But that evening when Pieter and I arrived home, Gunter was sputtering with excitement. 'Carmen affa loogad deese, ya crunks.'

He escorted us to the TV room, where Grant was already marvelling at what appeared to be around twenty empty Marmite jars, in varying sizes, arranged on the coffee table.

'Where did these come from?' I gasped.

'Outna blardy shet. Ve gorda shurploosh.'

'What do you keep them all for?' Pieter always tried to follow Gunter's logic to the end of its thread, knowing that whatever the destination, he'd be quoting it for days.

'Puddin schtoof in.'

For the next fortnight Pieter would respond to any question with 'Puddin schtoof in'.

'So what, you want us to take all these up to the pottery shop?'

'Taig da blardy lordoff 'em! Hif dat broot vants do vop dem orl up de bag passitch, e's *velcome* do dem!' That was Gunter all over. A few hours earlier he'd declared it a loadasheet and taken to the idea with a hammer. Now he'd somehow produced two dozen Marmite suppositories out of nowhere and was leading the charge.

During the day Pieter sold expensive suits at a department store in the city, I worked in the art department of an advertising agency, and Grant was based at the Department of Meteorology. Or, as Gunter put it: 'Pieter zells zoots, Dorny maksche der edverts, an Gherant's . . . oh, I dunno, soomsing do do vit der vetter.'

Violet's description was more revealing: 'That nice Tony, that nice Grant and the other one.'

One day I came home to find her a tad cheerier

than usual. She'd made herself a big plate of toasted sandwiches and was settling in for 'Da Soolimins'. 'I'm in a good mood today, Tony. Nothing can spoil it. Not even Gunter.'

She'd obviously heard the news. Pieter would be leaving us at the end of the week. 'No more monkey business. We're going to get another *nice* boy in here.'

'Diz dime I'm goona zee a lodda prorshpectiff carndidates. Ged zum deeshent booger wif hees het schcroot orn right.'

I retired to my room and collapsed onto, or rather into, my bed. The mattress was made of quicksand and left a person-shaped impression that lasted all day. There was such a bed in each of the three guest-rooms, along with an unevenly sprung armchair, a small writing desk, a large antique wardrobe and a chest of drawers. This latter item was the subject of one of Violet's more interesting quirks. If she came into your room and noticed a sock or sleeve or even the tiniest hint of fabric poking from a closed drawer, she'd discreetly point it out like someone informing you that your fly is undone. 'Drawer tongues', she called them.

'Tony, I think you've got some drawer tongues showing.'

'Oh, thanks, Mrs B.,' I'd say, returning the offending flaps to their respective mouths. 'That was close. Imagine if I'd had guests.'

'Don't be cheeky, Tony. You know I don't like drawer tongues.'

'Aww, *he-noof* vid der drorr tunks, ya zilly vorman!' As always, Gunter was out in the hall, looking for moths and listening in.

'What are you doing out there, Gunter? Shouldn't you be moving those ironing boards?' Violet gave as good as she got.

'Orright, orright, don' ged orl blardy 'schterical.' These little outbursts always drew them closer together and moments later Gunter, too, was in my room, wrapping his gnarled arms around his bride's waist and playfully butting her with his shining dome.

'Oh, Gunter, you've gone all silly,' blushed Violet.

'*I'm* da zilly voon? Dorny, vaddaya maygada "drorr tunks" bishness? Zhe's *matt*, init?'

'I wouldn't call your wife *mad*, Gunter.'

'Oh, don' voory, I vooden do dat. Zhe'd ligely da schtep me in me schleep!'

'Oh, Gunter!' shooshed Violet, wriggling from his grasp. 'You always say I'm going to stab you in your sleep. Why would I want to do that?'

'Vy not? Dat's ven *I'd* do id.'

Pieter would miss these two when he left, I knew he would, but they wouldn't miss him. I tried to picture his replacement, this 'deeshent booger wif hees het schcroot orn right'.

'What sort of questions are you going to ask them, Gunter?'

'Vedder day votch der nyoos, vor vun sing.'

'You think that'll weed out the nutters?'

'You jooz vait, Dorny. Der *broof's* in der *boodin*.'

The proof in the pudding arrived ten days later. His name was William Boyle, a wheezing walrus whose job involved handling medical waste. He was sweaty and talked to himself and had a ringmaster's moustache sprinkled with 'crarms'. But he did watch the news.

'Dorny, meet Villiam.'

He offered his hand. It felt like an eel. 'Villiam's moofink in dornight.'

'Got any smokes?' That was Boyle's idea of hello.

'Don't smoke, I'm afraid.'

'Ve don' lighe schmokink 'ere, Villiam.'

'Well, I'm sorry, Mr Baumann, but I'm afraid I *do* enjoy a quiet smoke every now and then. You didn't say nothin' in the interview about no smoking.'

'Oh, crarms.' Gunter looked at the ground and cursed himself for this oversight. Violet would be furious. She hated smokers and they hadn't had one for years. But William did watch the news.

'Hope this won't be a problem, fellas,' said Boyle, producing a packet of Camels from deep within his olive greatcoat. That's right, he already had some smokes of his own.

'Oh, gorsh,' said Gunter.

'Every now and then' turned out to mean every twenty-five minutes, and even if Boyle waddled right down into the street to spark one up, Violet would stand in the kitchen window wafting an oven tray. 'Disgusting habit, Tony. I can smell it from here.'

'Torknaloadasheet, vorman! Zo lorngass 'e dakezit down zere, I'm vine aboud id. Led da broot schmoke orl 'e vants do. May-pea 'e loosh zum blardy vate! 'E lorks like a farka-nellyphan.'

'No "F-words" at the table, please, Gunter. And don't call attention to William's weight. I'm sure he's very sensitive about it.'

'Shenshitif? E's a blardy monshter! Eden me outa howsh 'n' blardy home!'

With William eating us out of house and bloody home, schtoo shurplooshes were suddenly a thing of the past.

Somewhere in the twisted battlefield of Gunter's back yard, there was a fully operational chicken coop. He was keeping chickens ('vor de ex') and every morning, to the fury of our student neighbours, we were awoken by the cry of an 'ereusta' (rooster).

One morning the ereusta failed to sign in. He was gone. Not a feather remained. The obvious suspects were, let's see, *everyone within a three-block radius*, but no, Gunter had decided that Boyle must have eaten him.

''E's eden me blardy ereusta!'

'Gunter, listen to yourself,' I said. 'That rooster had many enemies. Why would Boyle want to eat him?'

'Orright, orright, may-pea nort. Leaf id.'

'You're sounding like a bit of a "crunk" there, Gunter.'

Gunter recognised himself for a moment and this sent him into a fit of rasping giggles. 'May-pea I shoot shearch ees rhume for beaksh,' he suggested, sending himself up.

'Sure, he wouldn't have eaten the beak,' I said, playing along.

'May-pea I shoot be jeckink ees schtoolsh for fedders.'

'Checking *whose* stools for feathers?' enquired Violet, looking up from a form guide.

'Don' blardy vorry, vorman. I'm torknaloadasheet.'

But the unfortunate turn the conversation had taken proved to be a disturbing portent.

The only remaining vestige of Pieter was his favourite jacket, draped from a padded hanger in my mothball-laden wardrobe. It was a grey, flecked, woollen single-breaster, the kind where you could roll the sleeves up to the elbow and instantly become the very picture of early eighties swingin' Auckland. Pieter had always accorded the jacket special powers and claimed that no woman had ever refused him anything, so long as he was wearing it. Now he'd passed it on to me. But the jacket's magic turned out to be completely Pieter-centric and I looked ridiculous, like Andrew McCarthy's retarded brother. As soon as Grant saw me modelling it, he collapsed like he'd been hit in the stomach by a high-powered rifle. 'Oh, fuck! Take it off, Martin. You're killing me.'

'I think I'm finally ready for some farny boogers.'

'Nah, mate, you look like Norman Bates. It's not working for you.'

'Damn that Malkmus! A note in the pocket says he wants a hundred bucks for it.'

'Pretend you never found it.'

'That's good!'

'In fact, pretend you never found the jacket.'

For Grant's amusement only, I continued to wear the jacket around the house. He, in return, would showcase the many colourful puffy ones he'd been stockpiling for the South Pole.

'Vot's goin' orn round 'ere, you boyce? 'Slika blardy feshion parate, init? 'Slike liffin wid a barn-cha blardy queerse!'

It was a Sunday afternoon and Grant and I were sitting in the TV room, relaxing in our jackets with Boyle, who had taken to smoking openly indoors in defiance of Violet's hastily scrawled sign. He was wearing an obscene brown towelling bathrobe that hung from his torpid form like a layer of molten toffee. Suddenly a familiar cry echoed down the hall. 'Oh, crarms!'

That was followed by 'Oh, Gherist!' (Christ) and 'Blardy broots!' Soon the speaker appeared, his face drained of all colour. 'Zum dishcushtink peek ash vorgorten do flarsh da blardy darny.'

Some disgusting pig had forgotten to flush the bloody dunny. Grant and I scanned the room for the most porcine candidate. The obvious suspect simply continued to spoon Coco Pops through his moustache, and remained focussed on the TV.

'Durn orf dose blardy Ronnees! Ve gorda ged do da bodoma deese.'

Grant leapt up and turned off the nature documentary. Gunter continued his inquiries. 'Zumbordy's gorda taig reschpornzibilidy for deese.'

'Flush it. Problem solved,' exhaled Boyle, with mannered disinterest.

'Leesin 'ere, Villiam, ef I find art itch you vot's nort flarshink dem turts, I'm gunna be ferry blardy pished orf. SO BLARDY FLARSH DEM TURTS!'

Gunter stomped off to his shed and I later heard the sound of jars being smashed in a bin. I realised that at no stage had I heard a toilet flush. Boyle's oversight was presumably still steaming up the mirrors in the bathroom. But he did watch the news.

Boyle merely sat there and very calmly dismantled his empty cigarette packet. He found the piece of silver paper and flattened it out on the coffee table. Then he slipped it into his pocket and scuttled out of the room.

Aside from the smoking and the nightly snack raids and the business with the 'turts', Gunter and Boyle managed to get along fine. In fact, one day Gunter emerged from his shed with a new invention he'd created, just for Boyle.

'Eedza hyooch blardy schigarette horlter,' he announced, and indeed it was. A huge bloody cigarette holder, fashioned from flexible plastic piping. It must have been a metre long. 'You boodit art da blardy vindow, an den yer can schmoke incite.'

Boyle was actually quite impressed. He wiped his hands on his ample gut and accepted the contraption as though it were Excalibur itself. 'Thanks, Gunter, matey, that's quite an effort you've gone to there.'

'Triad out, Villiam. Itch der beesh kneesh.'

But it wasn't the bee's knees. It was ludicrous. Because even if the cigarette itself was sticking out the window, surely you'd still be exhaling all the smoke into the room, as per usual? This quickly became apparent, but Boyle was so pleased with Gunter's gesture, he politely ignored the glaring design fault and insisted he'd be using nothing else when smoking in the TV room. Every night he swanned about, expelling exactly the same amount of smoke as before, but sending it on an extra metre-long journey beforehand. Ludicrous.

'Votcher dinker dat, Dorny? Nort bat, init?'

'It's just a really long cigarette holder. I don't get it.'

'He's right, Gunter,' agreed Violet, breathing through a cushion. 'It hasn't made any difference at all.'

'Aww, yer orla barncha blardy whinchers! Dat's es goot es vun you't get oop dere at Kayroat.'

As good as one *what* you'd get up there at K. Road? I hadn't seen anyone on K. Road selling metre-long cigarette holders.

Boyle and his new friend could get through half

a packet of Camels in an evening, and then, as always, he'd flatten out the silver paper and trot off to his room.

What was with the silver paper? Why was he hoarding it?

I remembered that back at primary school, when you didn't have anything for 'show 'n' tell', a piece of silver paper was like a get-out-of-jail-free card. If you couldn't produce a dead rat in a shoe-box or a packet of your mother's tampons, you'd just go, 'I've got this piece of silver paper from a Cadbury Top Deck', and you'd hear the next five kids screwing up their exhibits.

But why was Boyle stockpiling silver paper? Wasn't it weird enough that he handled medical waste? What was he up to?

Grant was the first to ask. He said there was no way he was going to the South Pole without knowing what was up with the silver paper. 'Hey, William, what exactly are you up to in Pieter's old room?' Grant still saw the room as Pieter's.

Boyle stubbed out his one-metre cigarette and shifted uneasily in his bathrobe, umming and erring. It was an impressive performance, but we could tell right away that he was dying to reveal all. 'All right, then,' he said, his eyes moistening with pride. 'Who wants to see me collection?'

Boyle led us into Pieter's old room, and I was surprised to find it clean and tidy. The bed was expertly made and there was nary a drawer tongue to be seen. He beckoned us over to the dark varnished wardrobe. It was identical to the one in my room.

'You ready?'

Grant and I exchanged a look that said, 'What was the name of that girl who disappeared up the Coromandel? The one whose body was never found?' Boyle adjusted his moustache, took a shallow breath and jerked open the door. 'Whaddaya think of *that*, fellas?'

Inside was an enormous ball of silver paper. A gleaming sphere, lovingly fashioned from hundreds, possibly thousands, of tiny flattened silver sheets. The man was insane.

'That's the collection?'

'That's just from the last four months.'

'This is what you've been working on?'

'Yep. Have to be some kind of record, don't you reckon?'

'I guess. I don't know of a bigger one.'

Grant and I had both just noticed that the diameter of the ball was wider than the door of the structure that housed it. Boyle's giant ball of silver paper was effectively trapped forever inside one of Gunter and Violet's wardrobes. But surely he could see that for himself?

'So . . . you're gonna keep going with this?'

'I reckon I can get it twice as big by Christmas.'

'Has Gunter seen it?'

'No, he hasn't. Let's keep this on the QT, fellas. Just between us.'

Just between us. The Fellowship of the Silver Ball.

Once Boyle had unveiled his 'Precious' and fielded the most obvious queries, an awkward silence descended.

'So, Boyle, this is . . . all silver paper? No tin-foil in there?'

'No!' he snapped. 'What are you suggesting?'

That night I lay slowly submerging into my mattress, haunted by the image of the shimmering silver orb cradled in the oaken womb of the wardrobe. It was merging with one of the first images I'd ever seen on television. Something from an episode of *Dr Who* when he was played by Patrick Troughton, in black and white.

The Yeti.

Seen today, the *Dr Who* Yeti are perhaps the least terrifying monsters in the history of science fiction. Imagine a pot-belly stove covered in fur. Now imagine it done really badly. But what made them so memorable was that each one had a square door built into the centre of his dark furry torso, and this door could hinge open to reveal the source of the Yeti's power.

A glowing silver ball.

Hardly the stuff of nightmares, but to a five-year-old who'd only just seen what a horse looked like, that was some freaky shit.

I lay awake thinking about it for hours. Gunter

and Violet didn't know it yet, but they were harbouring a Yeti. And that could only end in tears.

As the weeks went by, the source of the Yeti's power continued to grow. If you were, say, sitting on the front steps eating a chocolate bar, the second you dropped the wrapper, you'd hear a crinkling sound. By the time you looked round, he'd already be back in his room, adding it to the ball.

'You mon-keese might vorna glear art domorra. I'm gunna led orf a bomp.'

I had been there so long that the landlord's announcement that he was going to let off a bomb came as no surprise whatsoever.

'What sort of bomb?' asked Grant. He seemed genuinely interested.

'A bora bomp. Keel orl dem boras in one blardy heet!'

I would have thought the only reason the building remained standing was because all the borer had linked arms, but Gunter insisted some kind of indoor napalming was in order and had already purchased the necessary items, up at 'Kayroat'.

The next morning, everything was covered in old sheets and we all cleared out into the street to observe the termite pogrom from what we hoped would be a safe distance. Violet had organised a 'borer bomb picnic' in the front yard, and Boyle had already decimated the large tray of luncheon meat.

'So's there gonna be an explosion?' he burped, filling the air with a fine luncheon mist.

'Nah, chorl blardy shilent. You darnt shee or hear narfin.'

'So when's it over?'

'Takesch aboud shicks 'n' arf owwice.'

'Six-and-a-half hours? I'm gonna need me bloody smokes before then,' he complained. 'You reckon it's started yet?'

'I vooden go in dere, Villiam. 'Slike a blardy gash chame-per.'

Being in the TV room with Boyle was itself like being in a gas chamber. That room alone would surely have been borer-free. But there was no stopping him. He strode toward the house, his vast bathrobe billowing in his wake.

'Votcher blardy doin', ya crunk! You goona get gashed! Itch orl reedio-arctif!'

Radioactive or not (probably not), Boyle wrenched open the front door and barrelled into the swirling vapour.

'Oh, gorsh!'

Twenty seconds later he emerged triumphant, dusted with something lethal and waving a packet of smokes.

'I hope ya rhe-mempered do flarsh!' said Gunter. Even Violet got a kick out of that one.

'Piece of piss!' declared Boyle, brushing the deadly dandruff from his shoulders. 'Held me breath! Mind hosing me down?'

Grant and I declined this honour, and it was left to Gunter to train the garden hose on what can only be described as 'The Ponsonby Monster'. And Boyle was smoking the whole time. Because, as I now knew, he was protected by the mysterious power of the silver ball.

Just as the silver ball made it to a metre in diameter, Boyle got offered a job in Wellington working with a much higher standard of medical waste. He gave Gunter a week's notice and apparently requested that he be allowed to dismantle the front of his wardrobe, so that he might remove something which had become trapped inside. Boyle told me that when Gunter saw the silver ball he erupted in a fit of 'blardys' and started hitting him with a shoe. The debate continued until the day Boyle left.

'I just wanna take me ball with me! Is that too much to ask?'

'Dere shoodin' *be* a blardy borl in dere! Votchu *neet* a borl lighe dat vor, eny-vayce?'

'It's a project.'

'Pror-chect? You blardy *matt!*'

'I'm sure I can get the front off without damaging . . .'

'No,' said Violet firmly. 'It's too valuable.'

All that work. Boyle was inconsolable.

'Oh, don' ged orl shulky, Villiam. *Ve're* da vunce

schtuck vid der blardy borl! How ve gonna 'schplain dat do da negsch borter?'

'Seven months work down the fuckin' drain.'

And so William Boyle had no choice but to leave town without his giant ball of silver paper.

And Gunter, Grant and I hauled the Yeti out to the shed, where it was placed in a queue behind a three-storey birdhouse and a huge cabinet for storing empty jars.

But Boyle had one final mystifying surprise up his brown towelling sleeve.

Months – I mean literally *months* – after he'd moved out, a photograph of Boyle appeared in a local paper. In the picture he is seated at a window in a city office, demonstrating Gunter's metre-long cigarette holder. It is clear from the photograph that no stylist was present at the shoot, but Boyle sports a rascally grin beneath a headline that reads: 'Smoking goes out the window'.

'Da blardy booger! E's schtolen me blardy cornshept!' Gunter was ropable.

But that was the mystifying part. He hadn't. Here is the full text of the article:

SMOKING GOES OUT THE WINDOW

When William Boyle's cigarettes go through the window it doesn't mean he has given up smoking. The new look in cigarette holders was invented by Mr Boyle's landlord Gunther [sic]

Baumann because he was fed up with smoke-filled rooms. A resident of a small Ponsonby boarding house, Mr Boyle is always the centre of attention when he 'lights up'. His novel extension is made from plastic tubing and a dismantled cigarette holder. Certainly nothing to cough at.

Insane. Firstly, when they were taking the photograph, did no-one notice that the room was *slowly filling with smoke*? The headline should have read: 'Common sense goes out the window', followed by 'Insane charlatan demonstrates ill-thought-through concept and wastes everybody's time'. And secondly, he hadn't been 'the centre of attention' at the small Ponsonby boarding house in question for several months now, so why the hell would he claim he still was? In Boyle's mind, was he still living here with his big ball of silver paper? Whatever Boyle's intention, Gunter was quite chuffed to see his misspelt name in the paper.

'Crarms,' he said. 'May-pea I shoot ged round do eggstra-kaydeen dat borl.'

But Gunter never did extricate that ball. It remained imprisoned in the wardrobe, in the shed, until the day I moved out.

By the time I left Gunter and Violet's, I'd been there for sixteen months. Soon after Boyle's departure, Grant had headed for the Pole to await the release of the new U2 album, and none of the subsequent boarders remain in my memory.

I do remember my final day. I remember passing Pieter's magic jacket on to Gunter and I remember his response.

'I'm nord blardy veerin' dat! E's brorbably foola craps!'

I remember Violet inviting me to drop in for a cup of stew if I was ever back in town. She said it like she knew I wouldn't, like nobody ever did.

I remember an ill-fitting group hug, a final 'crarms' and one last reminder to steer clear of monkey business.

I'd miss them all. The crunks and the broots, all of them. But they'd be all right, I told myself. The Yeti would protect them.

I took one last look.

Gunter and Violet were waving from the top step. It was the first time I'd seen them standing like that, next to each other, as though posed for a photograph. But I had no camera and the moment was lost.

Twenty years on, all I have left is a copy of the article about Boyle's cigarette holder, a handwritten list of over fifty of Gunter's most popular sayings – 'Dose Ronnees' is at the top – and a single blurry snapshot of the house itself. Only when I look at these fading, fraying items can I be sure I didn't simply dream the whole damn thing. They are the only tangible proof I have. The rest is where it should be.

In der boodin.

breakfast in dubbo

Somewhere between Toowoomba and Dubbo the whole bus turned against me. All the passengers and even the driver, a pit-bull in short shorts and long socks, who'd run out of banter two k's out of Brisbane.

'I hope you're fuckin' happy, Martin,' he snarled, his trademark wit exhausted. I was seated a metre behind him, but out of habit he said it into the PA, giving the other sixty passengers another reason to hate me.

'You're not helping,' I whispered.

'No, *you're* not helping,' he informed the bus.

Which hurt, because I am nothing if not helpful.

Seven hours earlier, everything had been going swimmingly. I had two seats to myself at the front, which gave me a ringside view of the driver, Les

Mackie, in action. His monologue was well polished and he worked the microphone like a leathery Wayne Newton. He had a droll twist or lewd variation on every place name we encountered, Aboriginal or otherwise. Only Indooroopilly seemed to defeat him, although he may have been momentarily awed by the majesty of Indooroopilly Shoppingtown. He wouldn't have been the first.

As the place names became fewer and farther between, the scenery out the window changed from outer suburbs to flat, dry plains with the same blackened tree flitting past every fifteen seconds, Hanna-Barbera style. It was here that Les's material dried up, but from nowhere he produced two buckets of lollies and passed them back. Amidst the staggered crackle of lolly papers, conversations started breaking out all over, and within seconds I no longer had the luxury of an empty seat beside me.

'Mind if I sit here?' The voice came from a compact, sensible woman in a Ken Done-ish parachute ensemble. She introduced herself as Merilyn Toames from the Sunshine Coast and explained that her identically attired husband was falling asleep and she'd rather he had two seats upon which to do so. She soon spotted my New Zealand accent and this prompted her to reveal that she herself knew several New Zealanders, and that every last one of them was – get this – on the dole. I considered my response carefully.

'I should tell you that up until midnight next

Tuesday, I myself am what you might call a . . . Kiwi dole bludger.'

'Really? Oh, pardon me, but you seem like a nice enough person. These ones by us, they're . . . well, they're not exactly out there looking for work, if you get my meaning. They seem to spend most of their time lolling about on the beach, and there's always the smell of you-know-what drifting over the balcony.'

'Roast lamb?'

'Marra-jew-arna,' she enunciated.

'That sounds like New Zealanders, all right.'

'I'm sure they're quite harmless. They're simply unmotivated and, frankly, incomprehensible.'

'How do you mean?'

'One of them's always asking me if I want anything from the dairy.'

'The milk bar.'

'Apparently. Where do you milk your cows? At the sandwich shop?'

I'd heard this joke many times before, but I was impressed by the way she'd substituted 'sandwich shop' for the usual clumsy repetition of 'milk bar'. She'd made it work, but I had no way of knowing whether the modification was her own.

'Tell me,' I enquired, 'do they wear jandals?'

'Oh, yes. And jerseys.'

'It's a whole 'nother world over there.'

We paused for an announcement by Les, to the effect that there might be a very amusing sign coming up round the next bend, 'unless it's been taken down', which it had. After thirty seconds he gave up trying to remember what it had said, and instead passed back some Flake bars. Merilyn wrestled one free of its wrapper and resumed her enquiries.

'How long have you been on the ... unemployed?'

'Five weeks. But from next week, I'm cutting articles out of newspapers in Melbourne for two hundred bucks a week.'

'That's a job?'

'So they tell me.'

'And they need someone from ... interstate?'

'I'm a specialist.'

'And you're on your own?'

'My girlfriend's back in Brisbane. She's the one with the proper job.'

'What does she do?'

'She makes tiny cardboard buildings for an architectural model maker.'

'Goodness. Is there much call for that?'

'Oh, sure.' Brisbane was in the middle of a miniature real estate boom. She couldn't make them fast enough.

'And she's ... coming down with you?'

'Yes. In a couple of months.'

Merilyn chewed on this for a while.

'Right. So she's ... giving up her job as an architectural model maker to support you in your dream to cut articles out of newspapers?'

It was like something I would have said, but less smartarsey.

'Basically, yes. We're hoping the cutting-out will lead to bigger things.'

Despite the good humour, I could tell that Merilyn wasn't really sure about me. I did, in my early twenties, have about me the air of a geekish loner. My tragic collarless shirt and New Romantic-era trousers had already drawn several disapproving looks from the largely dressed-for-tourism horde behind me.

Her husband, Tobin, who'd made his money in 'extensions', had recently hit sixty-five, and although Merilyn herself was still in her mid-fifties, the pair had opted for early retirement and now spent their days roaming the country in buses and trains, subsisting on complimentary nuts and the endless, endless Devonshire teas. I couldn't imagine why anyone would voluntarily choose a tour bus as a way of traversing the country over and over again. It seemed to me that if you were always on buses, you'd eventually end up on the news, in some of that horrible footage of half a coach on its side and what looks like an entire retirement village strewn across the highway.

At some point in the conversation, Merilyn happened to mention that there was a movie scheduled for that evening. Of course. That explained the three TV sets clinging to the ceiling, equidistantly along the aisle.

'Do you know what it's gonna be?' I blurted, more excited by this prospect than I had been by any of the relentlessly magnificent scenery we'd been carving through for the last six hours.

'I hear we get to vote,' said Merilyn.

'Vote? What are the choices?'

'You'd have to ask Mr Mackie.'

I didn't want to appear too desperate, but the sad fact is that I am one of those people who, when boarding a plane, will have gone through the magazine and found out what the movie's going to be before most of the other passengers have reached their seats. As the iron bird begins its wondrous ascent and children cleave to the portholes to marvel at the ongoing miracle of flight, I'm the one going '*Krippendorf's Tribe*? How is that a "Special Event Presentation"?'

But a movie on a bus? That I'd never seen.

A couple of hours and several opportunities to purchase ammunition passed us by, and then Merilyn excused herself and returned to her assigned seat.

'Might see you later,' she whispered, squeezing in next to her unconscious husband.

'Nice to meet you,' I replied, although what I was thinking was: 'What's the movie gonna be?'

As soon as the Ken Done twins had been reunited, I tapped Les Mackie on the shoulder. 'Excuse me, Mr Mackie. I was wondering what the story is with the video tonight?'

'*Were* you, just?'
'How does it work? We . . . vote?'
'That's right. That way there's no arguments.'
'And how many titles are there to choose from?'
'There's four.'
'Can I ask what they are?'
'Well, that might give you an . . . unfair advantage.'
'What advantage? I'd still only have one vote.'
'Listen, I've had trouble before. People start lobbying each other for support for their title. Factions form. It can get quite ugly. Best you just find out tonight with everyone else.'
'Can I ask what genres?'
'No.'
'Are they recent —'
'Leave it!'
'Okay. Sure. We'll find out tonight.'
'Go back to your seat.'
'No worries.'
'There's a funny sign coming up.'
'Great.'
'Good.'
'Sorry about that.'
'Fine.'
'Is one of them *Ghostbust*—'
'Seat!'

With a rustle of synthetic fibres, Merilyn's husband, Tobin, settled his substantial self in the spare seat.

'Tony, is it? My wife tells me you're from across the ditch.'

''Fraid so.'

'She's nodded off, so I thought you wouldn't mind if I . . .'

'Not at all. Milky Bar?'

'*Mulky* Bar? No. Sorry. There's no end to the bloody snacks, is there? I reckon I'll go spare if he sends back any more "refreshments".'

I noted again that Tobin was wearing the sort of elasticated clothing that made this kind of trip so much more bearable. And there was no doubting his name, because it was felt-penned on an oval-shaped 'Introducing . . .' sticker, peeling slowly from his billowing tracky-jacket. 'What's with the sticker?'

'Oh, right,' he laughed, swatting it off with his enormous paw. 'That's from "Dancin' With the Oldies" at the resort last night. Not that I call meself an "oldie", but you've gotta get involved in the entertainments.'

'Speaking of which, have you heard about the movie?'

'Yeah, look, I'll be sleeping through it, whatever it is. Bloody rubbish, probably. The last two of these I've been on, it's been *Flashdance* or some bloody nonsense.'

'Will you still be voting?'

'Load of bloody carry-on, that's what it is. Who wants to watch bloody fillums when you're travelling through this kind of country? You might as well stay home if you just want to watch TV.'

'Right. You're not a film buff, then?'

'Don't get me wrong, I'm all for it. Me an' her, we go to the pictures a fair bit, but there's so much bloody swearing and language these days. Effing this and blinding that. We end up walking out half the time.'

'What was the last one where that happened?'

'*Caligula.*'

'*Caligula*? Why did you go to that?'

'It looked historical.'

Bob Guccione's *Caligula* was indeed 'historical', but not for the reasons Tobin was referring to.

'You know, I thought it might've been another *I Claudius*, but it was all bloody tits and genitalia. People's bits swingin' everywhere. It was like a smokers' night kind of a fillum. Much too blue for us, I'm afraid. I was very surprised to see Sir John Gielgud's name in the credits. Of course, you couldn't see him for goolies.'

'Maybe we'll be getting that tonight.'

'I bloody hope not.'

The possibility that the selection could end up being something as dire as *Flashdance* was really starting to weigh on me.

'Who cares what it is, anyway? There's more to life than bloody fillums.'

'Mr Toames, if you're really not going to take part, could I perhaps enlist your support in the vote?'

'Ooh, I dunno about that. What am I voting for?'

'We don't know yet, but every vote is going to count. Do you know if your wife will have any preferences?'

'You're having a lend, aren't you?'

'No, I just . . . I just think if we're going to have a film, it should be . . . the best one . . .' My voice trailed off as I realised how mad I sounded.

'Don't worry about it, mate. It's only a bloody video.'

'You're right. I know.'

'It's not the be-all and end-all.'

'No. Of course not. Forget about it. I won't mention it again.'

Besides, chances were all four titles would be shit. Then it would just be a 'lesser of four evils' vote.

As the sun began to make itself scarce, we pulled over to a rest area and Les Mackie crabbed his way up the aisle and into the curtained-off zone, where the second driver slept and presumably guarded the videotapes. Moments later, he emerged with a battered plastic tape-caddy containing the all-important selections in the popular VHS format. 'Got your pen and paper, everybody?'

He beamed with the largesse of a man about to reveal the contents of a very fat will. 'Tony, you writing these down?'

'I don't need to, Mr Mackie. Just hit me with the four titles.'

'All right – here we go, folks. These are the four titles you'll be asked to vote on, all of them courtesy of our very good friends at Video Kingdom, New Farm. First up we've got . . .'

This was it. Please don't let it be anything with Dom DeLuise.

'. . . *Beverly Hills Cop* with Eddie Murphy.'

Not bad. Not bad at all. A crowd-pleaser. Remember, this was the mid-eighties, in those magic months before *The Golden Child* and all those leather suits ended Eddie's incredible winning streak. We were off to a good start.

'Pretty funny stuff, but a fair bit of gunplay and swearing.'

What? Don't say that! In fact, don't say anything. Just read out the titles.

'Next up we've got *Excalibur* with . . . er . . . oh, look – I don't recognise any of these names, but it's a King Arthur kind of a thing. Pretty bloodthirsty, if I recall, but the music's not bad. There's a great bit with the theme from the Old Spice commercial . . .'

What the fuck are you saying?

'. . . and er . . . a little bit of what I'd describe as tasteful nudity . . .'

Good . . .

'. . . and a brief sequence of rutting.'

What? *Rutting?* Who uses the word 'rutting'? That

in itself is frankly more disturbing than anything in *Excalibur*.

'And I should warn you, there's one bit where a large black bird pecks the eyeball out of the skull of a corpse that's dangling from a tree.'

Except perhaps for that.

Between the pecking and the rutting, Les had pretty much eliminated *Excalibur* from contention. I could feel it in the air. This crowd wanted something with Bette Midler screaming at her husband, not corpses dangling from trees and the theme from the Old Spice commercial.

'Selection number three is one I haven't seen myself.'

Good. Hopefully there'll be no editorialising.

'It's called *Six Pack* . . .' Les scanned the cover.

What? What the hell is *Six Pack*?

'. . . with Kenny Rogers as . . .'

Did he just say 'Kenny Rogers'?

'. . . a washed-up stock car driver who finds himself in a mess the size of Texas when he inherits six mischievous orphans on the day of the big race.'

Did he just say 'orphans'? Mischievous orphans? And was there something earlier about stock car driving?

'That's untested waters, that one.'

Right, so obviously we're not going to be watching that one. What's selection number four?

'As is number four, which is a documentary . . .'

Documentary? I hadn't considered the possibility of a documentary.

'. . . called *This Is Spinal Tap*.'

Holy Bejesus! *Spinal Tap*? I didn't even know you could get it on video yet!

I'd seen *This Is Spinal Tap* in a one-off screening at Brisbane University the year before. There were about twenty of us in the audience and by the end we had all laughed so hard and so much that we could literally laugh no more. We staggered from the theatre in a daze. It was the funniest film any of us had ever seen. And the chances of anyone on the bus having seen it were virtually nil. It had never gotten a proper release and most people, if they knew of it at all, thought it was an actual documentary about an actual heavy metal band. Les Mackie was sitting on gold. *Spinal Tap* would bring the house down and it was pointless even to *entertain* the possibility of it being one of the other three. Not even *Beverly Hills Cop*, which surely everybody had seen, could compete with *Spinal Tap*. It was perfect. It simply had to be.

And they all fucking voted for *Six Pack*.

Perhaps I shouldn't have made the speech. But I wasn't the one who started it. As soon as Les had finished his spiel, a rather high-pitched woman right up the back stepped into the aisle and declared that 'the Kenny Rogers one' was the only one that sounded 'fit for family viewing'. Several elderly women chorused their support, but what they all failed to mention was the fact that, remarkably, there were *no children on the bus*! We were all adults here and surely we could handle the odd 'motherfucker' if it meant getting to watch a movie that was at least *halfway decent*!

The call for family values was echoed up and down the pensioner-controlled tube, with the odd half-hearted '*Beverly Hills Cop!*' thrown in for good measure. No-one wanted *Excalibur*, but to my astonishment there was one call for '*Spinal Tap!*' from a solitary beardo four rows back. I had at least one ally, but nowhere enough support to swing the vote. There was no other option. I'd have to make a speech.

'Les, if I could just say a few words . . .' I ventured.

'Who are you?' squawked an old bird down front.

'I'm a passenger,' I announced, seeing off any possible support I may have had, right there at the outset.

'And before we all decide . . .'

'I think we've decided, haven't we?'

'. . . I'd just like to put in a word for *Spinal Tap.*'

Boos. There were boos.

'It's a documentary!' someone spat in apparent disgust.

'No, it's not,' I attempted. 'It's a comedy, a really funny comedy, *disguised* as a documentary.'

'What piffle!' someone snorted.

I realised I'd made it sound too high-falutin'.

'Who's in it?'

Shit. I couldn't say 'Christopher Guest' or 'One of either Lenny or Squiggy'. 'Meathead's in it!' I said, in clear desperation.

'Who?'

'Meathead, from "Archie Bunker". And he directed it.' That didn't help.

'Billy Crystal's in one scene!' I was flailing.

'Who?'

This was before *When Harry Met Sally*....The next comment, seemingly from Norman Bates's mother, cleared up the confusion.

'The gay one from *Soap*,' she hissed, triggering a wave of disapproving tongue-clicks.

I had one final gambit.

'Patrick Macnee's in it! You know, "Steed" from *The Avengers!*'

'What, in a heavy metal documentary?' said a skeptical fat bloke. 'You're talkin' through your arse, mate!'

He was quickly admonished for his 'arse'.

'Listen to me,' I pleaded. 'It's incredibly funny. It'll be *so* worth it, I promise you.'

'*Six Pack*! Let's have *Six Pack*!'

'Kenny Rogers!'

I fully expected someone to start a chorus of 'You Picked a Fine Time to Leave Me, Lucille'.

'Hey, I like Kenny Rogers,' I said, as convincingly as I could. 'But don't you just get the feeling that *Six Pack* is going to suck?'

Apparently, nobody did. But I had nothing to lose. 'I mean, does *anyone* remember it coming out at the movies?'

'I don't remember *Spinal Crap* coming out at the movies,' contributed someone, and sadly '*Spinal Crap*' did get a laugh.

'How about this?' I suggested, my welcome long since worn out. 'We put on *Spinal Tap* and if, after ten minutes, nobody's laughing, we'll turn it off and put on *Six Pack*?'

'But what about the language?' said the original speaker, returning to her theme.

'There's a *little* bit of language, sure, but it *is* funny and as there's no children here . . .'

'"Lick my love pump"!'

It wasn't a helpful interjection, and I couldn't help but notice it came from the mouth of my one supporter. He was grinning from ear to ear. But Les Mackie wasn't amused.

'What did you just say, young man?'

He repeated it, adding 'It's one of the funniest lines from the movie. From *Spinal Tap*.'

Cue mischievous orphans.

During my pathetic entreaty, I'd seen Tobin and Merilyn Toames slowly but surely lose all respect for me. To them, I was now 'The Mad Guy Who Tried to Make Us Watch a Disgusting Documentary About Cocksucking'.

I slumped sulkily in my seat as Les fired up the video, in order that Kenny Rogers and his wholesome brood might cleanse us all of the filth that thin man with the New Zealand accent had ushered aboard this otherwise family-friendly perambulant.

Six Pack began predictably enough, with tracking difficulties. After Les had pulled over, fixed it and rewound, we were treated to the title sequence a second time. This featured Kenny, in a hairstyle so altogether ludicrous that it just had to be real, piloting a pick-up truck through the countryside. As he drives, Kenny's character, the washed-up stock car driver, listens to the radio which is playing a song... by Kenny Rogers! For a brief hopeful moment I expected that the film would feature a scene where Kenny's character and the real Kenny meet up, via the magic of early-eighties split-screen. But no, it remained an unexplained movie coincidence that a song by Kenny Rogers was being enjoyed by an anonymous everyman *who happened to look exactly like him*!

As one unsurprising occurrence blandly followed another, there descended upon the bus the warm calming glow of PG familiarity. It was like any Disney Movie of the Week, with haystacks and wisecracks and plaid shirts and a jaded but lovable good ol' boy ready for redemption, and a montage, at the hands of those crafty but warm-hearted orphans, on the day of the big race. There seemed very little likelihood of anything offensive happening, beyond possibly the title song, performed live, in a bar scene, by its author.

Then, about ten minutes in, something happened that nobody could have predicted. It was Kenny's first scene with the orphans. He was rescuing them from a river – don't ask – when the little one, the most mischievous one, turned to his bedraggled rescuer and said: 'Mister, you look like *shit*!'

It was like we'd hit a roo. But no-one could say anything, because this was the movie they'd settled on. This was the one they were going to have to stick with, no matter what. And besides, perhaps it was a one-off. Or a mistake. In 1986, *South Park* was still a decade away, and in movies children didn't say things like 'You look like *shit*!'

Or 'holy shit!', 'holy shit!', 'arse', 'bastard', 'chickenshit', 'holy shit!', 'sonofabitch!', 'no shit, Dick Tracy!' and 'holy shit!!!' – all of which quickly followed in the initial *shit*'s disgraceful wake. This was the most foul-mouthed moppet in the history of cinema. Even Kenny was powerless to stop him, although he didn't seem to notice it 'til around the seventy-minute mark, and even then he earned a pointed 'chickenshit!' for his trouble.

It was around here that Les Mackie announced to the bus: 'I hope you're fuckin' happy, Martin.' Thus, instantly upping the swearing ante, and undoing what little work Kenny's misty-lensed final act 'change of heart' was doing to stem the torrent of infant-generated abuse.

'Only the Kenny Rogers one . . .'
'*Chickenshit!*'
'. . . sounds fit for family viewing.'
'*Arse!*'

As the end credits rolled, and the real Kenny Rogers belted out another reason not to buy the soundtrack album to *Six Pack*, the bus fell silent. Nobody said anything for several dark kilometres. The evening had been ruined. And it was all that guy up the front's fault.

When we were awoken, around four in the morning, Les had been replaced by the other driver, fresh out of the packet, and unaware of the *Six Pack* affair. He announced to the semi-comatose crowd that we would be stopping for breakfast at the finest breakfast restaurant in all of Dubbo.

Like zombies after a big night on the tear, we shambled into the blindingly bright aquamarine breakfasting area of a restaurant that seemed to be constructed entirely from aquariums. We were about to chow down on breakfast, at four in the morning, amid dazzlingly lit denizens of the deep in Dubbo. It was like we were dreaming breakfast. No-one was saying anything, but as I queued for plastic cutlery I began to sense a distance from the other passengers that was something more than the haze of interrupted sleep.

I'd only been trying to help. And now, no-one

wanted to sit with me. As I huddled over my dishwasher-hot bowl of cold milk and Rice Bubbles, and shimmering reflected fish-shapes danced across my empty table for ten, I recalled the words of a man who had once said:

You got to know when to hold 'em,
Know when to fold 'em,
Know when to walk away
And know when to run.

unlucky 12a

If there's a funnier spectacle than that of an elderly Hasidic Jew in the full get-up, swearing and kicking and punching an ATM with one hand, while holding a fast-melting ice-cream cone in the other, I think I'm yet to see it. The physical assault on the handibank was merciless and did nothing for the old Jewish stereotype, but the ferocity of the attack was offset by the care with which the gentleman balanced his frosty vanilla treat. When it became apparent that the rain of blows was having little effect, he stopped, muttered a final Yiddish obscenity and turned, as startled to see me as I was by the single blob of ice-cream on the end of his nose.

So this was the suburb which at least two acquaintances had evoked with the phrase 'boring as batshit'. The incident I had just witnessed suggested that some strains of batshit were more interesting than others, and as the old man wandered away, cursing and licking, I wondered whether this was a sign of things to come.

There were twenty-two flats in the two-storey, U-shaped block. The exterior had been painted a hideous baby-kak mustard, which perfectly complemented the stench of Maggi chicken noodles that permeated every corner of the building. The only touch of near-character upon the entire ochre brick façade was a cheerfully slanted wrought-iron signature, reading 'Sycamore Court'. Someone had painstakingly hand-painted this legend in Liquid Paper on all twenty-two of the block's wheelie-bins, presumably to distinguish them from those of the identically designed but contrastingly labelled 'Eucalyptus Close', located opposite.

My first-floor flat was positioned between number 12 and number 14, but in keeping with the rampant medieval superstition that characterised the mid-1980s, the plastic number on the door read '12a', rather than '13'. That the small 'a' was clearly a reversed number '6' lent my flat the air of a handicapped student, struggling to keep up with the others in his inverted plastic calipers. I wasn't happy about this, but rather than invite the satanic cataclysm of bad luck that would apparently result from correct numeric sequencing, I instead reassured myself that my flat was somehow 'special'.

Which it wasn't. It consisted of the usual four rooms and a balcony that could comfortably accommodate a single fat man holding his breath, assuming that was your idea of entertainment. The walls were painted off-white, which gradated to off-yellow as the eye rose to the ceiling, suggesting that the previous tenant had been that bloke from the *Guinness Book of Records* with fifty-two lit cigarettes crammed into his mouth. Only after I had moved in did I discover there were no picture hooks anywhere, and to attach even one would require a written appeal to the landlord. Even the new miracle product of the day, Blu-Tack, was forbidden, according to a sign attached to the kitchen wall. Attached with what, I never did ascertain. Not that I had anything to exhibit. Or sit on, as my only item of furniture was a queen-size mattress. A rented TV filled one corner, and the traditional stolen milk-crate full of LPs sat, unplayable, in another. As there were no closets, my pathetic-even-by-eighties-standards clothes were stored in two open suitcases. The only visible decoration was a free Valhalla Cinema calendar, which, in accordance with the rules, was laid out flat on the floor of the loungeroom. Any visitor to 12a would have to assume the occupant was an out-of-town assassin whose next hit was due to take place during a screening of *Betty Blue* or *Eraserhead*.

Or more accurately, an unemployed New Zealander, miserably waiting for his girlfriend to save enough money to move down from Brisbane. She'd know what to do, how to get round the draconian Blu-Tack decree. Until then it was just me and the pigeons, whom I believed had come to rely on the handfuls of breadcrumbs I confettied from my kitchen window every morning at ten. A harmless-enough routine, I thought, but there would be repercussions later. As it turned out, it would take a lot more than a couple of plastic numbers to defuse the curse of flat 12a.

Access to my quadrant of the mustard monolith was via a glass security door, affixed to which were three fraying stickers. One warned potential intruders that a StrongGuard Security System was in place. This was not true. The landlord had invested only in the stickers. Another insisted that we were all involved in some kind of Neighbourhood Watch scheme, which was also not true. The third sticker, to everyone's mystification, was one urging us to 'Vote for Barrie Unsworth!'. Unsworth was a man so singularly unmemorable that today even he would have difficulty recalling that he was once Premier of New South Wales. But we were in Victoria. Maybe this was where his re-election campaign went wrong.

Inside the door was a small purple-carpeted foyer containing a single bucket of sand, a tiny back-beach for cigarette butts. One pissing-down Monday evening around seven, I had arrived home and was standing in the foyer shaking out my sodden umbrella when I heard a familiar rasp.

'Is that you, Mr Martin?' It was Norma from number 10.

'Yes. I'm just on my way out.'

'I'm coming down.'

There would be no escape.

'I need to ask you something.' Norma, a widow in her early sixties, was a wiry polyester dynamo who moved like a carpet shark. Her fragrance was Peter Stuyvesant and her complexion Jack Palance. I liked to imagine she was a former crime matriarch. A long-term inmate at Sycamore Court.

'You use the laundry, don't you?'

'Yes.'

'At night?

'I have done.'

'Have you seen anything . . . funny . . . going on in there?'

'Funny?'

Norma leaned in close, her mouth a lipless slit permanently curled with disapproval, as though every conversation were an unwelcome distraction from the fags. 'Last night a member of the body corporate disturbed a naked man, crouched behind the dryer . . . manipulating himself.'

'Manipulating himself? What . . . emotionally?' Who could resist?

'Fiddling about. Downstairs. You know what I'm talking about.'

More than she could ever imagine. 'I'm sorry, I haven't seen anyone. When did this happen?'

'It's happened twice now. Last Tuesday and last night.'

'Have the police been called?'

'They came last week, but who would have thought he'd strike again?'

'Well, why hasn't anyone caught him? He's nude and preoccupied. Couldn't one of your members have tackled him?'

'What a disgusting thought.'

'Surely it's not going to happen again. He'll have moved on.' To stickier pastures.

'Perhaps so, but in case he hasn't, the body corporate has agreed on a plan and we'd like everyone to join in.'

Join in? Until this conversation I had never heard the term 'body corporate'. Who were these people?

From a Coles plastic bag, Norma produced a small aerosol can-sized klaxon horn. 'We want everyone who uses the laundry to take one of these – that way if you discover this person, you . . . set it off. I won't demonstrate because . . .'

'Sorry, how does this work? You want me to take that horn with me to the laundry?'

'Yes. Everyone's got one.'

'And if he's in there . . . going at it . . . I fire this off?'

'That's right.'

This was the plan? 'And what happens then? Obviously I'll have thrown him. He'll lose his place. But then what?'

'Well, we all come down and we catch him.'

And even if that unlikely scenario occurred, what would we do then? Lead him to the body corporate's wicker man?

The klaxon sat on the kitchen bench as I stood at the window, flinging breadcrumbs down onto the path outside the laundry. I had decided that rather than buy into Norma's insane horn plan, I would simply stop using the laundry at night. Let the alleged nudist enact his lewd manipulations behind the dryer without my interruption. I did wonder what the appeal was; the lino in the laundry was dusted with Omo crystals which would, I imagine, make for an irritating work-surface.

Still, even that sad fucker was getting more action than I was. And the couple in number 12 were getting more than all of us. How could I know this? Because one day they raced past me on the stairs, giggling and fumbling and very obviously on the verge of desperate undress. I entered my flat moments after they entered theirs, and by the time I'd collapsed onto my mattress, the stereo at number 12 had been cranked up to a cup-rattling volume.

The song: 'Midnight Blue' by Lou Gramm. That's Lou Gramm from Foreigner.

Midnight blue,
Whoa-oh-oh,
Midnight blue.

That was followed by fifty-five minutes of silence and then, at the same volume . . .

Midnight blue,
Whoa-oh-oh,
Midnight blue.

I'd love to report that still audible beneath the whoa-ohs was the unmistakable sound of hot sex, but that would be a lie. The walls may have been too solid or the hot sex too subdued, but it had to be one of those because there was *no fucking way* two people would race home like that just to listen to 'Midnight Blue' at top volume, and then listen to it again fifty-five minutes later. And two more times later that night. And at least once, sometimes three times a day, for the next five weeks straight. Not even Lou Gramm would do that.

Whoa-oh-oh,
Midnight blue,
Yeah!

For the record, the song was never played twice in a row, which suggested the couple were winding things up within its 3.40 running time. For that is the running time. I checked.

But they weren't my only musicologist neighbours. On the other side, at number 14, lived Wendy someone, a bubbly, pocket-sized, fortyish lesbian with a shore-leave haircut and an unfailingly chipper manner. 'How's it hangin'?' she'd enquired as she shook my hand – so effusively that the only possible response was 'Straight and true, ma'am'. Wendy's stereo was set to a lower volume than The Foreigners at number 12, as I had named them, and I would often hear her belting along to 'Drop the Pilot' by Joan Armatrading. Now, the first couple of times this can be quite charming, in a 'You go, girl!' kind of way. But after a week of . . .

Drop the pilot, try my balloon,
Drop the monkey, smell my perfume,

. . . enough was enough.

Drop the mahu, I'm the easy rider.

That was it. That was the line that got me. 'Drop the mahu.' What the fuck was the 'mahu'? Pilot, sure. Monkey, fine. But mahu? I couldn't find it in the dictionary. Was it a made-up word? I had to know, but this was pre-Google. Perhaps Wendy knew – she always seemed to give the 'mahu' an extra kick. I mean, you wouldn't give a word like 'mahu' such pointed emphasis if you didn't know what it meant . . . would you?

My flat was the meat in a mahu–'Midnight Blue' musical sandwich, and there on the floor lay my crate of vinyl records, dumbstruck and unavailable, the stereo being at that time approximately 2600 kilometres to the north. At the front of the crate, staring back at me, was my then-favourite album, *Rain Dogs* by Tom Waits. How I longed to return fire and blast the neighbours with a bit of 'Cemetery Polka'.

Uncle Vernon! Uncle Vernon!
Independent as a hog on ice!
He's a big shot, down there at the slaughterhouse,
He plays accordion for Mr Weiss!

Try fucking to that one, Foreigners! It can't be done. I checked.

Two weeks had passed and the horn had still not sounded. I assumed that the fiddler's season at the Court had ended, but Norma maintained that it wasn't over until the fat lady came. Not in those words, of course, but she did strongly urge that we remain vigilant, klaxons at the ready. Reminders were included in the monthly body corporate newsletter, a one-sheet circular edited and distributed to all twenty-two letterboxes by Norma herself.

Along with a sober editorial on wheelie-bin etiquette and a request that all tenants donate to the klaxon fund, May's issue of the *Sycamore Branch* made passing mention of 'The Snowdropper in 12a'. Now this, I must stress, was in reference to my daily blizzard of breadcrumbs, which it seemed the body corporate had judged to be up there with suspending bras from your balcony. Although I too am against the latter, as I find it creates an unwelcome 1974 *Man About the House* vibe and before long you're shouting the word 'Bristols!' and popping next door with the ice-bucket. But what was wrong with feeding a few pigeons? Aside that is, from the miniature sense of megalomania the act bestows upon the feeder, as though one were delivering a vital Red Cross parcel to a cluster of speckled refugees. But that was hardly an editorial matter.

And what was with 'The Snowdropper'? Perhaps Norma was unaware of the term's colloquial definition: one who steals women's underpants off the clothesline. Not an occupation you'd list on your tax return, but apparently a group large and committed enough to have earned themselves a baffling descriptor. How underpants-theft equated to the generation of snowfall was anyone's guess, but I was sure that if I tried to explain this to Norma, it would only make things worse. In next month's *Branch* I would amusingly be referred to as 'The

Kiddyfiddler', because someone had seen me playing the violin with a baby goat. An unlikely scenario, granted, but one still likely to produce something more pleasing to the ear than 'Midnight Blue'.

At first I panicked. Would everyone now refer to me as 'The Snowdropper'? What if one presumed perversion led to another? Before long they'd have *me* pegged as the crouching laundry onanist. Every time I'd leave my flat, someone would fire off a horn and I'd be swooped on by members of the body corporate, armed with flaming torches made from old copies of the newsletter. On the other hand, nobody read the *Sycamore Branch*. You'd see tenants putting it straight into the bin, because it was largely a shopping list of Norma's personal gripes, dressed up in official-sounding lingo. Bicycles in the foyer were 'restricting egress'. Wheelie-bins not lined up in correct sequence were causing the row to be 'numerically compromised'. 'No Junk Mail' signs on the letterboxes – 'There needs to be a "one in, all in" policy' – that was one month's 'Hot Button Issue'. Another time the newsletter ran with the lead headline: 'Who's Cooking Cabbage?'. Those who actually read the thing in its entirety had all come to the same conclusion: Norma needed to be killed.

I could never work out why the couple playing 'Midnight Blue' every five minutes were never demonised by the *Branch*, the way 'The

Snowdropper', 'The Bin Switcher' and another favourite, 'Mr Urinates-Too-Loudly', were. Perhaps Norma herself was taking prurient delight in the couple's Gramm-scored exertions, and therefore turning a blind eye in the pages of her organ. Even the editor of a one-sheet newsletter can be subject to a conflict of interests.

It was Friday afternoon and I had just returned from a job interview I knew had gone badly from the moment the interviewer started snoring. I was standing in the foyer knocking back a Ventolin and restricting egress when I heard what had become a familiar greeting. 'Snowdropper!'

It was Hutton, from number 5. Always in the hallway in pyjamas, like it was his house. A nice enough bloke who once got me to hide his tiny dog, Nuts, in my flat, five minutes before his landlord was due to arrive for an inspection. He later told me the landlord had come across a dog turd in the kitchen and Hutton had tried to tell him it was a plastic one. The plan, and the turd, fell apart when the landlord asked him to prove it.

He trotted up to me with uncharacteristic urgency. 'Mate, can you smell that?'

'Smell what?'

'You'd better come and see what they've done.'

Hutton loped up the stairs and I followed, feeling like someone about to be asked to identify a body.

'Someone's tried to break into your flat. I think I disturbed 'em.'

If he hadn't, the pyjamas would have.

'Check it out.'

A person or persons had tried to wrench off my doorknob using, it appeared, some sort of heavy-duty claw. There were deep, jagged gouge-marks all around the metal knob and it was twisted to one side, rendering it useless. They didn't get in, and now neither could I.

'Can you smell that?' There was a faint scent of burning metal in the air, like we'd just missed a fireworks show.

'They've used some sort of power tool.'

'A power tool? Wouldn't that be kind of . . . loud?'

This was bizarre. How did they even get through the security door?

'I heard something. I thought it was tradesmen.'

'Did anyone else hear it?'

'I think they waited 'til the song started.'

'Song? What song?'

Midnight blue,
Whoa-oh-oh,
Midnight blue.

Oh, get fucked. No way! They couldn't have planned the whole thing around the song. It had to have been a coincidence. And why my flat, out of the twenty-two? I tried to imagine the conversation, had the break-in been successful:

'Gentlemen, when I said we'd do one last job before we retired, I didn't think we'd hit the God-damn motherlode!'

'Everyone round the crate. Brains, hold up the Valhalla calendar. This is one for the history books [flashbulb].'

'Now, let's get this show on the road. Les, grab an end of the mattress. I hope you've all got your passports!'

As it later transpired, the 'Metal Claw Bandits' had been pulling off doorknobs all over Melbourne. And, as Hutton had demonstrated, the very noise their device created acted as a cover because surely it could only be tradesmen. It was perfect. They probably wore overalls and had a van with the word 'Acme' on the side.

I used Hutton's phone to call for a locksmith, but as his 'earliest window' was at nine the next morning, I would be locked out of my flat all night. Maybe I could sleep in the laundry, behind the dryer. What could go wrong there?

'Snowdropper!' said Wendy, having flung open the door halfway through my knock.

'I need to climb from your balcony onto my balcony,' I said. 'I've been locked out, by burglars.'

She led me into a flat filled with so many candles and scarves and velvet throw-pillows that Stevie Nicks could have shot her next album cover there. 'Herbal tea?' she offered, predictably.

'Not in this lifetime,' I replied. 'Do you have Nescafé Blend 43?'

As it happened, Wendy shared my sophisticated taste in instant coffee, and so she set to work, searing the granules like a pro. 'So, you on your own next door?'

'For the time being.'

'Meaning?'

'Girlfriend's in Brisbane.'

It was like one of those Nescafé commercials, but with a nerd and a lesbian. But for the first time in weeks I had someone I could whine to, in person, and as the Blend 43 turned to cask wine, out came the war stories. Wendy was in the printing trade and when she referred to herself as an 'inky-fingered lezzo', I collapsed in tears of drunken laughter and realised I was in no condition for the climb.

'What's she like, your girlfriend?'

'She's an artist.'

I loved being able to say that. It was so much easier to talk about her than to speak of my own recent success as someone who wrote 'tags' for radio commercials. That bit at the end of the ad where a different voice says something like, 'This Saturday night at The Dingley Powerhouse, supported by Nick Barker and the Reptiles.'

Boldly, I asked Wendy about her girlfriend and she showed me a photograph of someone who looked remarkably like herself. In the picture, the couple were dressed as The Blues Brothers and appeared just to have heard the funniest joke ever told. They were currently apart, as the girlfriend, some kind of animal husbandry midwife, had been sent to New Zealand on assignment. When I asked where precisely, Wendy came out with a question Australians just love to ask, and always with a tiny hint of sarcasm. 'Where are those boiling mud-pools again?'

'You know full well where they are.'

'I think she's there.'

'She wouldn't be anywhere near there.'

'What *is* it with the boiling mud-pools, anyway?'

I'd lived in New Zealand for twenty-one years and never once visited the boiling mud-pools. Why would you? All they do is bubble and smell terrible. It's hardly Dream World. There's a kiosk where you can buy a plastic ruler with a picture of some boiling mud on it. And a triangular felt pennant reading 'I visited the boiling mud-pools!' which prompts only the question, 'Why?' There were kids in my class who had visited the boiling mud-pools and they all rated it just below a visit to the dental nurse.

This led Wendy to ask me if I'd heard the album from Neil Finn's new band, Crowded House. Before I could answer, she'd dropped the needle on the opening track.

She came all the way from America,
Had a blind date with destiny,

And the sound of Te Awamutu,
Had a truly sacred ring.

She cut the volume. 'What does that mean? Te Awamutu?'

I explained that Te Awamutu was a town I used to drive through every weekend and, while an excellent spot, I couldn't recall any 'truly sacred ring'. A truly enormous furniture warehouse, sure. But a truly sacred ring? Of course, it's the *sound* of Te Awamutu the song is alluding to. I do remember the sound system in the Te Awamutu cinema being pretty good. That was where I saw *The Bounty* and it was the first film where I noticed the sound being all around us in the theatre. Every creak of *The Bounty* could be felt and every wave washed up and down the dozens of tiny speakers that encircled us. It was everything Sensurround was supposed to have been ten years earlier. It was so good that several people vomited, mostly children, and the stench was so overpowering that after fifty minutes, the matinee screening was aborted. Half an hour later I returned to the cinema to find an usher bracing open the fire door, but you could still smell the spew and inside a ferocious argument was in progress. The usher caught my eye and raised a weary hand.

'You don't want to go back in there, mate,' he warned. 'Someone skidded on some chuck and it's turned into a bit of a stoush.'

Aah, *The Bounty*. Those who survived it still recall its bitter sting.

Some people don't laugh at stories about vomiting, but Wendy wasn't one of them. She had several of her own. And after a few more drinks, I felt like we knew each other well enough for me to ask the question I'd wanted to from the moment she'd let me in.

'Elephant driver.'

'What?'

'It means "elephant driver".'

'How do you spell it?'

'M.A.H.O.U.T. Mahout, pronounced "mahu".'

'Bugger me.'

As the empty glass slipped from my hand onto the rug and I sank back into the capacious corduroy couch, Wendy leaned in close and said, 'I know what you need.'

'You do?'

'It's obvious.'

'My girlfriend?'

'Your stereo.'

We were each right and two weeks later, both arrived on my doorstep. It was a great day, and that night we made beautiful, noisy love. To 'My Sharona'.

'I'm telling you, it's because of the pigeons.'

It hadn't taken my girlfriend long to notice that everyone in the block now addressed me by my nickname. She was forever planting her underpants in my stuff and then 'discovering' them just as I walked in. 'You think I don't know what you're up to?' she'd say. 'You filthy little snowdropper!'

For three days everything was fine. Everyone wanted to get a look at the Snowdropper's missus and she revelled in her fleeting celebrity status. She eagerly awaited her first appearance in the *Sycamore Branch*.

'Perhaps I'll be "Lady Snowdropper". Or the "Snow Queen"!'

'Maybe they'll have a contest. You could be next month's "Hot Button Issue".'

We were a team again, spinning our bullshit and going about our lack of business. And with furniture and music, cell 12a finally became flat 12a. All was what passed for well.

But as night fell on day three, a new sound arrived to freak us right out. 'There's something moving in the walls! Aaaahh!'

I'd heard those panicky girlish squeals many times before. They were mine.

'What are you saying?'

'There's something in the walls, moving. Like a rat, but . . . bigger.'

'Maybe it's the masturbating guy.'

'Listen!'

It ran up the rear wall of the bedroom, on the inside, leaving an unseen mist of rubble-crumbs scattering down the bricks behind it. Then it scuttled across the ceiling, followed moments later by a second one. It was like I was back on *The Bounty*.

'Possums! It must be possums!'

'Inside the walls?'

'They're like squirrels.'

'What?'

What was she talking about, squirrels? I ran to the window. Nothing. Just the moonlit frontage of Eucalyptus Close staring back at me. I wondered if exactly the same thing was happening over there. As always, my girlfriend had the answer.

'I think we should call "Peter the Possum Man".'

'Peter the Possum Man' was booked out, as was 'Paul the Possum Man'. Sadly, the possum disposal listings in the *Yellow Pages* contained no 'Mary' and the promotional opportunities such a confluence would have afforded went unrealised. We settled on 'The Possumnator', whose slogan was 'They won't be *baack*!' He turned up two hours late and failed to see the humour when I suggested he travel back in time to when he was supposed to have arrived.

'So how do you do it? How do you catch them?'

'Mate, you don't wanna know. You two stay put.'

Wow, he really was The Possumnator.

'I'll be back in two jiffs.'

Didn't he mean *baack*? As far as I knew, killing possums was fun but illegal, so I assumed he was going to lay some traps. But that wasn't his plan at all.

Now, I don't know whether it was because he was running late, or whether this is just standard practice in the possum game, but all he did was ball up a lot of chicken wire and use it to plug up the building. I followed him down and that's what he did. Ball up sheets of chicken wire into impenetrable blobs and stuff them into the five potential entrance points. Unaware that I had been observing him, he returned to 12a and presented us with his invoice.

'So . . . what have you done with them?'

'They won't be bothering you again.'

'Because they're . . .?'

'Out of the picture.'

Out of the picture, but were they out of the building? After he'd departed in a van filled with nothing but chicken wire, I dragged my girlfriend downstairs to view his handiwork.

'What if they're still in there?'

'They can't be in there. He wouldn't do that.'

'He can do what he wants. He's the Possumnator.'

'They must live in a tree during the day.'

'Wouldn't the tree be the place to be during the night? Night-time, that's when you see possums balancing on the powerlines. During the day, that sort of thing would look too showy. Surely that's when they're back in their cosy little apartment. And now they'll be in there forever, entombed, like Jack Thompson behind that fireplace in *The Evil Touch*.'

'No! He must have released them.'

'There was no releasing. It was all chicken wire.'

That night we lay in bed, staring at the ceiling, alert for the scratch or scrabble that would confirm our worst imaginings. It came at 10:41. Our screams would make the newsletter.

Eventually the smell became so bad, we had to move out.

We sat in a borrowed car, across the road from Sycamore Court, and waited for the sound Hutton had promised us. It was two weeks after our departure and, at his invitation, we had returned to witness an experiment. There was something we had to know.

'BWAAAAAAAAAAAAARRRMMP!'

It was a sound no-one in the block had heard since that day, months earlier, when Norma had originally distributed the horns. Hutton, like us, had longed to see exactly what would happen and who would respond. Now we would witness the body corporate's vengeance in all its startling haste and choreographed splendour.

'BWAAAAAAAAAAAAARRRMMP!'

Still no-one came.

'BWAAAAAAAAAAAAAAAAAAAAAARRRMMP!'

After a moment, the balcony door at number 12a slowly slid open and the new occupant emerged.

He was small and hairy and wearing an apricot bathrobe, opened to reveal a large pair of white Y-fronts. He looked around, searching for the source of a sound only he, of all the tenants, would not have understood. There would be many more to come.

prang

'There's no fuckin' way them lights were on when you drove past!' slurred the man who'd just nearly killed me.

In fact, my lights had been on, but his hadn't as he'd shot out of a driveway and knocked me into the gutter. He'd only clipped the tail of my tiny Honda Civic, part of which was still spinning in the street, but the impact had left me stunned and tasting blood in my mouth. His bull-barred black tank was barely scratched, but an alarm was squealing, and had the driver not been entangled in his seatbelt, he would have been staggering over to blame me for the whole damn thing. For even before he'd freed himself from his vehicle, he'd rewritten the accident six ways from Sunday.

'Them lights weren't on! No fuckin' way! You

can't blame me for this! What were you thinking? This is bullshit! I never even saw you! What the fuck are you trying to pull? I've got lawyers, you know!'

'My lights were on.'

'Bullshit! You just turned them on then!'

He finally escaped the safety belt, took one step and fell flat on his face, the fall possibly broken by the can of beer in his jacket pocket. 'This is bullshit!' he said, from the footpath.

'The lights were on,' confirmed my girlfriend, stepping from the Civic like someone arriving at a premiere.

'This is fucked,' concluded the gentleman in defeat.

Details were exchanged and our none-too-sober assailant promised to sort it all out with his insurance people. As he stumbled off to find a cab, we congratulated ourselves on our cool under fire. We had been like husband-and-wife UN negotiators reasoning with a crackhead. It had ended well, and we had his address and phone number. And his name: Darryl Heineken.

There was, of course, no Darryl Heineken. And the address didn't exist. And the phone number was for a massage parlour. It was as though the events of that evening had never happened. Or would have been, had my girlfriend not Nancy Drewed Mr Heineken's ass. She had written down the tank's licence plate number, and the next day we found ourselves down at the local police station describing the bloke.

'Like Tom Selleck when he doesn't have a moustache,' offered my girlfriend, referring to the star of the then-popular *Magnum P.I*. Although I had always believed that comparing suspects to actors and TV characters would be the best way to obtain an accurate description of a felon, I felt a 'tacheless Selleck was wide of the mark.

'Remember the guy in the yellow jacket at the end of *Blue Velvet*?' I said. 'Just standing there, frozen to the spot. Shot in the head, but not actually dead, his police radio still crackling in his yellow jacket pocket.'

It was as I said the words 'his police radio' that I felt a sharp change in room temperature. After an awkward eternity, the policewoman spoke. 'We can't just give out addresses. We'll follow this up ourselves and get back to you. Have a nice day.'

The chances of that happening were slim to bugger-all, because I was absolutely furious. Furious that we had been tricked by a drunk and furious that my yellow-jacket-guy comparison was, minus the head-wound, dead on the money and that this would never be acknowledged.

Back at the car we sat contemplating the investigation we had set in motion. Would it all end up in court? Would I have to buy a suit? Would I finally get to realise my dream? The one where I leap from my chair before a packed courtroom and shout, 'That's a lie! A damn stinking lie!'?

Of course not. There would be phone calls and paperwork, estimates and assessments. Replies awaited in due course for reasonable periods and sums totalling. The above-mentioned acknowledged and the below-mentioned forwarded immediately, on completion of same. Our reference, their quote, Yours faithfully and furthermore. That's what we were in for. Weeks of that bullshit.

I hit the ignition and we drove off in silence, the rear bumper rattling and scraping behind us.

'We've found your Mr Heineken,' said the voice. 'He's very apologetic. It's up to you how far you want to go with this.'

All I wanted was the 1500 odd dollars it was going to cost to restore my vehicle to the pristine shitheap it had been before. I wrote down the man's name, which turned out to be Leo Belletty.

'Leo Belletty speaking.'

'Hello, my name's Martin, you drove into —'

'Martin! I've been trying to chase you up.'

'Yeah, there was some . . . confusion about the details you gave us the other —'

'Yeah, look, I'd had a few, although I wasn't over the limit. I must've given you my old address.'

And his old name, presumably.

'Whatever. How do you want to proceed with this?'

'All right, straight to business, is it?'

'Sorry, did you want to . . . what?'

'Nothing! I'm just saying, why don't we get together, you and me, and sort this out in a civilised manner?'

Was he proposing a duel?

'How do you mean?'

'Well, what are you doing right now?'

What I was doing was wondering whether this bloke could possibly sound any shonkier. I had a feeling that if we did get together, I'd be coming home wearing nothing but a barrel, as he drove away laughing, in my car.

But I agreed to meet him, at his flat in East St Kilda, which he described as 'a temporary arrangement'.

Leo Belletty's temporary arrangement was situated in a quiet cloister of bohemian apartments, hidden and protected from the roar of the nearby Nepean Highway by a huddled congregation of trees. The offending vehicle was parked out front, and stood out like a sore one from the 3RRR-stickered bombs that crowded the forecourt. I peered through the driver's side window and saw three crumpled beer cans scattered on the passenger side floor. Leo had made no attempt to clean up the scene of the crime. I figured he must have other things on his mind.

He was waiting for me at the door. 'Come in,' he said. 'It's all temporary.'

Leo was as I remembered him, but now in focus

and in control. He wore grey slacks and a white shirt with the sleeves rolled up and a loosened tie, like the harried editor of a small-town newspaper. He swept me into his lounge, the contents of which appeared just to have been delivered. A new couch had erupted into a new bed, a new TV and sound system was already up and running, and there was packing plastic and bag-ties all over. Several fine suits lay draped across a brand-new dining setting, and on the new coffee table was the biggest ashtray I'd ever seen, a bottle of Scotch and a packet of condoms. I froze. Was Leo planning to seduce me?

'Sorry, mate, ignore the frangers. I'm still gettin' me shit together here. You married?'

I replied that I wasn't and he gave me a nod which suggested I was somehow a smarter man than he. 'They get you in the end, mate. And this is where you end up. Out on your arse.'

Even before I'd heard the ugly details – and I had no doubt that they were about to come out – something told me that the man standing before me had possibly contributed to his own sad predicament. Perhaps it was the frangers.

'I'm not saying I wasn't partly responsible for the marital malaise, as it were, but there are, as you know, Martin, two sides to every story. Drink?'

Truth be told, 10:30 in the morning was a tad early for me, but I decided that the more I could stay on-side with Temporary Leo, the more likely I'd be to see my 1500 bucks. He glugged a morning measure of whisky into his glass, knocked it back, filled mine, and then filled his again.

'Here's the thing about your car,' he said. 'I know a bloke.'

Uh-oh.

'I know a bloke who can fix your car for cost, and that way we can keep the insurance companies out of this.'

'What bloke?' I said, with unforced cynicism.

'Nah, nah, nah, don't be like that, mate! He's legit. Affiliated. I can't say who with 'cos it's under the table, but it's one of them big joints that has blokes in white coats fixing your car – you know, like the fuckin' Ponds Institute.'

'And who pays?'

'I do.'

This made no sense at all.

'Why would *you* pay? Why not get the insurance company to pay?'

Leo set up another shot.

'The car's in me wife's name. I'd have to contact her, and things are bit iffy at the moment.' He emptied the glass in one quick move, then braced himself for a peptic kickback. Once the pain had passed, he added, 'It's all a bit iffy in that regard.'

'And you'd pay 1500 bucks . . . '

'Seven hundred, 800 tops, through my bloke.'

'Just to avoid calling her?'

'Mate, don't make me show you a photo. She's a ballbusting bitch.'

Every such insult would be followed by a tortured admission of partial complicity.

'I'm not denying there have been indiscretions. Certain indiscretions. I'm away on business a lot of the time, in Asia, if you get my meaning. There has been the odd transgression, and as a result a lot of hurtful things have been said, and thrown. But both parties are at fault. She's done certain things herself, I'm sure she has. I could hire a detective if I wanted, sticky-beak into her affairs. Dig up some dirt. Who knows what I'd find? But I like to think I'm above that sort of thing. Having principles, I call it.'

And who was I to argue? I hadn't been to Asia for an odd transgression.

It occurred to Leo that his tumbler was empty again, so he checked his watch. Satisfied that he was keeping pace with whatever drinking schedule he had set himself, he set the glass on the coffee table, and began searching through his various jacket pockets for the one with the cigarettes.

'So, how do we wanna do this, mate? You bring your car here?'

We agreed that I would drop my car at his flat the following morning and that he would take it from there. That way, everyone was sweet; me, him and the ballbusting bitch.

My girlfriend didn't like the sound of Leo, his arrangement, the frangers or any of it. We had taken responsibility for this, she reminded me. If anything went wrong, we couldn't go crawling back to the proper authorities. I accused her of busting my balls and she snorted, pointing out that had I been in possession of any, I would have come home with a cheque for 1500 dollars.

'This way is better,' I insisted. 'He's getting it done for cost.'

'By who again? Guys in white coats?'

'He knows a bloke.'

'Hmmm.'

I knew that 'Hmmm' well. An arthritic removalist and a travel agent working out of her house had been our most recent 'I know a bloke' disasters. But this time it would be different.

That was what I was telling myself as I handed Leo my car keys the next morning. He was just on his way to whatever it was he did. He was carrying a leather satchel, a suit bag and a Tupperware lunchbox containing an apple and a packet of cigarettes. I had removed my house keys from the key ring beforehand, as I always do with my mechanic, because I feel paranoid taking them off in front of him. Even though the act merely says, 'I'm taking these off because I need them to get into my house,' to me it always feels like, 'I'm taking these off because if I don't, you'll be straight round to my house to rip me off.'

Leo took the keys from me with his teeth, and deposited them onto the passenger seat.

'So, when will I hear from you?' I enquired.

'Before you know it,' he promised.

Now, while the phrase 'before you know it' tantalises with the magical implication that normal time constraints are somehow being circumvented, it doesn't offer the security of 'tomorrow afternoon around four'.

'You'll call me when it's ready?'

'If I had a car phone, mate, I'd be calling you now.' He revved the tank, honked his horn and was gone. I looked down and found, to my surprise, that I was not wearing a barrel.

Three days had passed and Leo still hadn't called. I rang his flat and discovered he had invested in an answering machine. The message that came with the machine apologised for its new owner's absence and, feeling no rapport with its generic persona, I opted not to leave a reply. Instead, I would pop round to Leo's in person. From behind the fridge I fished out the Met bus timetables I had forsaken since I'd bought my car a year earlier. But all the schedules had since changed and it was like learning to walk again. I'd forgotten all the little moves and overshot my stop by five blocks, like an amateur.

Arriving at Leo's block, I was surprised to find my car parked out the front. I was even more surprised to see that nothing had changed. The back left-hand corner was still stoved in and the car was parked exactly where I'd left it. He'd done nothing. Somewhere, on the other side of town, an 'I told you so' was being locked and loaded.

There was no sign of Leo's car, so I didn't bother knocking. The venetian blinds were open and I could see that he'd finished unpacking; everything was in its place. There were records, but from across the room I could identify only *Skellern Sings Astaire*, an album every one of my mother's friends seemed to own. On the coffee table I could see what looked like a brand-new James Clavell paperback and an empty wineglass. A poster full of footy fixtures was stuck to the fridge, and three empty pizza boxes were stacked neatly next to the bin. It was a fully operational bachelor pad. But where was the bachelor?

That night I called Leo's machine and this time I did leave a message. It was fairly blunt. Two days later I returned to Leo's flat, at sundown. My car was still unmoved and, through the blinds, I could see that everything was as it had been earlier in the week. The same empty wineglass sat next to the same unopened paperback and the stack of pizza boxes had risen no higher. He'd gone away. Leo Belletty had done a runner. But he knew I needed my car. He'd be back. He'd be back before I knew it.

Leo was gone for twenty-eight days. An entire month. He returned to find that his answering machine contained a double album's worth of increasingly abusive material, and there was more to come when I finally cornered him in what now looked like a permanent arrangement.

'Calm down, Martin. You look like you're gonna have a fuckin' asthma attack.'

'Where have you been?'

'Let's just say that everything has fallen very nicely into place. The missus has seen reason and decided to settle things amicably. She'll be keeping the house; I'll be moving in here with Stacey until the baby's born.'

The baby? I pictured some knocked-up nymphet from the typing pool. 'But where have you *been*?'

'Fiji.'

'What?'

'I've been investing in my emotional future.'

'You've been on holiday?'

'Listen, you're the winner here, because this now means the damage can be covered by the insurance company.'

'Sorry, how am I the winner here? You were supposed to get my car fixed a month ago! I've had to fucking rent one to get to work!'

'Don't let's get all dramatic here, Martin, the insurance'll cover that as well. Christ, I thought you'd be happy for me.'

'What?'

'I'm at a crossroads here.'

'Good for you. Hope your lights are on.'

The Fijian sabbatical seemed to have erased any memory he had of the accident that had brought us together. He was plunging headlong into his emotional future and I was an unwelcome remnant of a history he had now disowned.

'So, what am I supposed to do now?'

'This is now a matter for my wife. She's taking delivery of the vehicle tomorrow. I'll give you her details. I'm getting a Porsche.'

Of course he was.

I never saw Leo Belletty again, but now there was the testicle-hating wife to deal with. I called her and she sounded as though Leo had half-explained it to her while she was half-listening. But the prospect of sorting out one of her soon-to-be-ex-husband's messes seemed a familiar one, and she wearily invited me round to help her fill out the forms.

Maria Belletty may well have been a ballbusting bitch, but that wasn't the impression I got. She was a tall, slightly posh mid-fiftyish dame, with a mischievous smile and a hairstyle known, even then, as the 'Robyn Nevin helmet'. She opened the door and led me into the world Leo had so decisively escaped. It was a beautiful split-level home that looked to have survived several noisy childhoods.

Maria sat me at the dining room table, sparked up a menthol, and listened, with some amusement, to my account of the accident. She roared at the line,

'I've got lawyers, you know!', as if she'd heard it many times herself. When I described where this had all happened, she rolled her eyes and asked me if I'd met 'her'. I told her I hadn't, and she proceeded to describe someone much older and fatter and stupider than I had imagined. Someone much more manipulative and ugly and likely to screw him for every penny and then he'll come crawling back, than I had pictured. But this was all expressed with a lightness and humour, like she was quite happy with the way things had turned out.

She wasn't giving much more away as we tackled the forms over tea in cups of thin, fine china, but she seemed willing to do anything to make sure I was fully reimbursed. She had a contented smile on her face the whole time, as if this were a most pleasant dress rehearsal for the signing of her own divorce papers. I thought about what Leo had said, how he could have hired a private detective, if he'd wanted, to sticky-beak into her affairs. Dig up some dirt. Who knows what he'd find? I considered asking Maria for her side of the story. I could have mentioned the frangers or the massage parlour and got the whole sordid picture out of her. But I like to think I'm above that sort of thing. Having principles, I call it.

the doctor is out

If you live in Australia, and you happen to make it known that you're afflicted with a back problem, it's only a matter of time before you hear these words: 'Shagger's back, is it, mate?'

When this happens, I generally like to smile and offer a shrug, leaving open the possibility that yes, it just might be shagger's back and when will I ever learn? But this time the attack had been triggered not by intercourse, but by a single sneeze. A sneeze sufficiently powerful to effect some kind of vertebrae misalignment and leave me curled on the floor, wailing like a Yoko Ono album being played at the correct speed.

'Shagger's back, is it, mate?'
'No, it fucking is not!'
'What do you need?'

THE DOCTOR IS OUT

'I need crunching. You're gonna have to do it.'
'What?'
'Sit on me. I need you to sit on me.'

Inviting someone to sit on you is never easy, but on three separate occasions in the early nineties, this is precisely what I had to do. One time the service was performed by a large Greek taxi driver in the back seat of his idling cab. As I recall, he was giggling the whole time – and left the meter running.

This is understandable. To someone who has never experienced the sudden searing distress of a spasming spinal cord, the request that you mount the victim as you would a chaise longue can seem both preposterous and a tad forward. But if executed correctly, this move can *click-click-click* the relevant vertebrae right back into place, like tumblers in a safe. Then you've made a friend for life.

My back-crunching years stretched for a decade-and-a-half, and during that time thousands and thousands of dollars were spent on an endless loop of physios, osteos and chiros. People who sit on you for a living. Drugs were administered and I was karate-chopped and acupunctured and strapped to some kind of Black & Decker Workmate-style table which stretched my spine one vertebra at a time, after which someone came in and rubbed Vaseline on my back and then I was electrocuted for several minutes. And rather than report this to Amnesty International, I simply signed the forms and promised to pop back next week for more of the same.

Year after year of filling out the form on the clipboard and being ushered in to meet yet another back-boffin, with yet another medieval torture-rack and the well-practised expression of someone who's heard it all before.

'Well, Doctor, the pain starts here and shoots right up to here. I've been told I have a mild scoliosis, and that causes a displasure just here and consequently up here, even if I'm lying down.'

'Right. Shagger's back, is it, mate?'

Dr Bentley's clinic wasn't like the others. He was the seventh chiropractor I'd been to in as many years, and up until then they'd always been cloaked in the trappings of alternative medicine. Typically, the chiro would be one of many healing enablers, co-existing in an oil-scented, brown-rice enclave, where the receptionist – not that you'd call her that – always looked like Jennifer Jason Leigh in an amateur production of *Hair*. Most of the rooms were located in Clifton Hill. The gentle, holistic atmosphere always belied the jarring violence of the manipulations performed within. For no matter how thin, bearded and lentil-fuelled the therapist may have seemed, he or she was still capable of producing from your spine a sudden startling ratchet sound that could be heard down the hall. The result was an instant, genuine sense of well-being and a bill you couldn't claim on.

THE DOCTOR IS OUT

Dr Bentley was one of those other chiropractors, the ones who look like proper doctors and whose names appear on brass plaques rather than in the back of *High Times*. His clinic was eight to ten album tracks from the inner city, in a normal suburb where anyone who looked like a hippie would have been dragged behind a ute through the local business park. Bentley Chiropractic was on the ground floor of a three-storey building so anonymous that the people who worked there would be hard pressed to describe it without stepping outside. It was a big box of 'suites', with a small circle of shivering smokers loitering by the entrance, like inkstained seagulls.

The doctor shared his annex of the module with a small urinalysis laboratory. The Pissworks, I called it.

'Imagine working there all day. You'd always be wanting to go, I reckon. You'd be excusing yourself all afternoon. Or maybe you wouldn't, 'cos they'd always be needing more to work with in the lab. Anyone for a top-up?'

Dr Bentley's receptionist didn't appreciate being used as a try-out audience for bad stand-up material. She handed me the clipboard and said: 'They're very nice people over there, you know.'

I'm sure they are, but you wouldn't shake hands.

'And it's not really what it sounds like, urinalysis.'

Not really what it sounds like? What, not really the analysis of urine? 'What is it, then?'

'It's all computers. They're like accountants.'

Yeah, right. Accountants with splash-guards.

As I hunched on the frankly uncomfortable chrome-and-black-leather couch scratching away at the forms, I resolved never again to commence a discussion involving urine with a woman I'd only just met. But when you come across someone who spends eight hours a day facing a glass door through which the only thing visible is a large sign reading 'Urinalysis', you have to say something.

For some reason, the chiropractor's form always requested that you identify your 'religious beliefs'. If you chose not to answer, the chiro would soon find out anyway, from the name of whatever deity you screamed upon receiving his first 'adjustment'. Dr Bentley's form dispensed with such spurious enquiries, demanded only basic facts and quickly got to its main reason for existing, which was boldly to invite you to FORGET EVERYTHING YOU KNOW ABOUT CHIROPRACTIC! At first this struck me as a desperate plea, as in, 'Forget everything you know about chiropractic. This never happened. You were never here.' Then I remembered Dr Bentley wasn't going to be like all the others. That's why *I was* here.

My six previous chiropractors had used every magic crunch in the book. They'd played me like a *Flintstones* xylophone for year after year, with nary a hint of one of those mishaps you see on *Today Tonight*. They'd all been recommended by friends with renewed posture and revivified marriages. I had no complaints. Then, one public holiday in an unfamiliar city, I had been forced to seek out the services of the only back expert working that day. He turned out to be the chiropractic equivalent of that bloke who fixed the Joker's face in the first *Batman*.

As part of a paid engagement too ludicrous to describe in detail, I had been required to jump from a height of two-and-a-half metres onto a solid concrete floor, five or six times in quick succession. Contorted into the shape of a question mark, I leafed through the *Yellow Pages* with my tongue. The only available chiro recognised my symptoms immediately and within half an hour I was lying flat on his kitchen table, receiving treatment I can only assume he learnt at a party while drunk. The question mark became an ampersand, and I was flown back to Melbourne under cover of morphine.

Upon recovery, I vowed never again to go the crunch. When my next attack occurred two weeks later, I finally fished out that card I'd been given for a man who would make me FORGET EVERYTHING I KNOW ABOUT CHIROPRACTIC! A man who used a different, more American technique, one originally designed for use on victims of car accidents. People who don't want to be sat on.

'Mr Martin, is it?'

Dr Bentley was the biggest chiropractor I'd ever seen. Easily six foot five, his head was the size and shape it would be in a wildly exaggerated newspaper cartoon. He was fully bearded, 'tached up, and solidly bald in a manly Ed Harris kind of way. He wore a cold grey suit that could only have been obtained Where the Big Men Buy, and which was visible beneath a white dustcoat large enough to provide all-weather protection for a Howitzer.

'Dr Bentley.'

His hand enveloped mine and the FORGETTING began.

'I can see you're in some pain.'

'I thought I was disguising it.'

He laughed the laugh of a kung fu master to his foolish young apprentice. 'I think we should step into my office.'

His office was like that of any GP, but with subdued lighting and a near-subliminal bed of rainforest sound effects playing on a loop through invisible speakers. Dr Bentley was as stiff and formal as his lighting and sound were dreamy and relaxed. And combined with his unwieldy desk and awkwardly framed certificates, the impression was that of an enormous tax accountant forced to set up temporary premises in a relaxation therapy clinic with an unlocatable CD player.

'Now, before we start, I should tell you, I won't be doing any of that spinal manipulation nonsense.'

This was what I had hoped to hear. It was time for the manipulation to end. But what would replace it?

'It's a complete waste of time anyway, because it does nothing to treat the *cause* of the problem.'

'Excuse me. Should I go through my history of—'

'No point. I can see it all, right here in front of me.'

'Really?'

'You shouldn't have your legs crossed, you know.'

'I know. It's actually more comfortable this way.'

'That's what you think.'

I got the feeling that at some point he would start hitting me with a ruler.

'You've seen this, I'm sure.' It was the old plastic see-through human, that poor generic bastard who stands in for all of us during embarrassing anatomical discussions.

'Yes. That usually comes out.'

'You've heard how everything's interconnected, how it all comes back to the spine?'

'All bullshit, is it?'

'It's actually very true.'

'So I shouldn't forget *that* part?'

'I'm sorry?'

'Never mind. Interconnected, you were saying?'

'Interconnected. You've heard all this.'

'Yes.'

'But have you *felt* it?'

'The . . . interconnectedness?'

'Let's get you horizontal.'

It was a line that had never worked for me.

Dr Bentley showed me to the table. The one with

the hole where your face goes, like a pile-bloated arse on one of those inflatable cushions. He broke the seal on the sanitary toilet-seat-cover-for-your-face, gently positioned it and directed me to assume the position.

'You want me to leave my shirt on?'

'Your shirt, Mr Martin, is completely beside the point.'

I would have to start working on one of those lines for myself.

'Hands loose at your sides, please. Don't forget to breathe, and turn your head to the left, if you could. That's good. Now to the right, please. Yes, that's as I suspected.'

'What? What did you suspect?'

'Quiet, please. Raise your left foot ever so slightly, if you could. That's it. Now the other. And relax. Did you notice that?'

I had noticed nothing, except that he had produced what looked like a nail gun.

'Just relax, you'll feel a sharp tap, nothing to worry about.'

K'pok. It felt like nothing more than the surprise tap of one of those tiny hammers the doctor will use on your knee, in a procedure possibly designed solely for his own amusement.

'And the same again.'

K'pok. This time lower.

'And you can stand.'

'What? Already?'

'Try it.'

I stood up straight and for one unnerving moment it felt like I was leaning over at one o'clock.

'Does it feel like you're leaning over?'

'Yes. Why is that?'

'Because you're actually standing up straight.'

'What have you done?'

'I've basically tricked your nerves into releasing their grip on certain of your vertebrae.'

'You've *tricked* them?'

'Pretty much.'

'How long will it feel like this?'

'I want you to walk around the block for twenty minutes. Do *not* sit down. Do *not* get into your car. I'll see you again in a week.'

Dr Bentley had tricked the nerves, all right. He'd led them a merry dance. And I'd worked out how he'd done it. It was as though he'd loosened some invisible ropes that were fastened tight around my torso, making it easy for the vertebrae to slip back into place of their own accord. Unlike my already FORGOTTEN earlier chiros. They had crunched the vertebrae without even touching the 'ropes', which soon contracted and pulled everything out of whack again.

Dr Bentley's gorgeous nurse led me back to the gorgeous receptionist, and I stepped into the gorgeous carpark, *didn't* get into my car, and set off on my twenty-minute road to recovery. This was good. This was different. This was expensive, sure, but it was non-violent and it really seemed to work. I walked ever more upright for enough blocks to pass by three separate Tatts Pokies venues. Three blocks, I think it was. By the time I made it back to my car, I had decided beyond any question to make Dr Bentley my regular chiropractor.

His campaign of trickery continued for the next fourteen months. My nerves were deceived, misled and flat-out lied to, time and time again. If my back locked up, he would gently release it, like it was one of those Chinese finger-traps that respond to lightness rather than force. I imagined that he would never have trouble with a seatbelt sticking. Occasionally, if I suffered a twinge at the weekend, I would lie flat on the floor of the loungeroom, pathetically trying to direct my girlfriend to recreate one of the doctor's mysterious manoeuvres. It never worked. Maybe we needed that CD of rainforest noises.

Dr Bentley never mentioned women, but a small framed photo of a very attractive one clutching a flame-haired toddler was propped on his desk, and a standard crayon depiction of a house, dog and tricycle was taped to the back of the door. I did, however, learn that his favourite TV shows were *Yes, Minister* and *Rumpole of the Bailey*. He liked 'any film with Alan Rickman' and couldn't imagine a funnier night out than *Four Weddings and a Funeral*. He was an ABC-FM man and a regular at the opera, who occasionally dabbled in a bit of 'amateur G&S'. He was one of those classic Australian white men in their mid-fifties for whom anything British is quality, while anything American is automatically rubbish. Except Bilko and Sinatra. On Frank, at least, we agreed.

He was quite chatty when discussing film, TV and music, and like me, seemed to have nothing to contribute to the vast Australian sporting debate, whatever that might be. But personal enquiries made him tense up, to the point where I would come close to suggesting he call his own receptionist to arrange an appointment.

'Dr Bentley, can I ask, how long have you been doing this?'

'Oh, look, about fifteen, twenty years.'

'Where did you start out?'

'Um, you know . . . I'd rather not talk about that. That's kind of personal.'

'Sorry.'

'And you can stand.'

'Thanks. Round the block?'

'Twenty minutes. *Don't* get into your car.'

'Course not. What sort of car do you drive, out of interest?'

'You're an inquisitive one, aren't you?'

'Sorry. It's just . . . you're an intriguing person.'

'I'm not, you know. You ask the girls.'

'Are you on with them, by the way?'

A pause.

'That's one of your jokes, isn't it?'

'Yes.'

'Next week, then?'

And I was the one who needed loosening up. It was odd that someone who spent all day releasing the knotted stress from the many tightly wound city folk who filed into his rainforest, was himself such a tough read. He could tell you what kind of day you'd had from the way you'd sat in his chair, but he himself was closed for inspection.

One time I bumped into him, outside of work, in a bookshop in the city. He was on his own and didn't seem to know how to talk to me away from the controlled lighting of his therapy suite. After an uncomfortable, 'No, you go' greeting, we both found ourselves at a loss for words. Suddenly, just as he was building up to a 'Well, goodbye, then', I grabbed a large hardcover book from a display stand and placed it on my head.

'Check this for posture,' I began, but it had already slid off and hit the floor with a loud 'plap', which, in the monastic atmosphere of the tiny bookshop, got everyone's attention and caused Dr Bentley to go quite red. By the time I had returned the book to its plastic triangle, he had fled the store, without another word.

When I saw him at the clinic two weeks later, it was as if the bookshop encounter had never happened.

'So, what have you been up to, Dr Bentley?'

'Nothing. I've been away.'
'Really? Where abouts?'
'Rather not say.'
'Fair enough.'
K'pok.
'And you can stand.'

I knew something had happened when the nurse led me into Dr Bentley's room, did the thing with the face-protector herself and told me to mount the table. 'Doctor will be with you in a moment.'

She left the room, and I lay there wondering what had happened to the doctor's beloved protocol. No handshake, no preliminary chat at the desk, no 'Let's get you horizontal.' After a couple of minutes, I heard the door open and in limped the doctor.

'How are you today, Tony?'

'Good, apart from the usual,' I muffled, from the pile-cushion.

It wasn't until the head-turning, foot-raising and nail gun had worked their usual sorcery, and I could stand, that I saw it. Dr Bentley was wearing a neck-brace. A tasteful one, in subdued autumnal hues, but a neck-brace nonetheless. And not a small one.

'Don't ask.'

'You know that's not gonna be possible.'

'Please.'

'What happened?'

'There was an accident.'

'And?'

'This is the "and",' he said, gesturing to the contraption.

'But . . . you were still able to . . .'

'Oh, I can still work. But it's . . .'

'What?'

'Well, it's not a very good look for . . .'

'A chiropractor?'

'You know I don't like to use that word.'

'What, here at Bentley Chiropractic?'

'Can we never mention this again?'

'We've barely mentioned it at all.'

'I know, but can we not?'

'Sure. I'll add it to the list.'

Two weeks later and the brace was still on. And the doctor himself looked like he hadn't slept for a week. After reminding me, as always, not to get into my car, he sat down and when he realised I wasn't allowed to, quickly stood up. There was an awkward announcement to be made. 'I'm afraid I'm having to . . . take some time off.'

'The neck?'

'Partly.'

'How long for?'

'Six months. Maybe a year.'

'Right. Okay then.'

'I'll give you the card of a bloke over in Ringwood. He's on the same page with all this.'

'Well, you look after yourself, Dr Bentley.'

'I'll see you in a year.'

'Let's hope you don't forget everything you know about chiropractic.'

'You know, Tony, if I could laugh, I still wouldn't.'

'I'll be off, then.'

'Here, take these.' He handed me the large cardboard envelope full of X-rays I had handed him a year earlier.

'You haven't even looked at them, have you?'

'I never do.'

That was more like the Dr Bentley I knew. I left him sitting at his desk, alone with the twittering birds and insects of the Amazon basin.

During Dr Bentley's year off, I didn't once visit the bloke in Ringwood. I'm sure he was very good. I guess I simply didn't want to believe that anyone else could live up to Dr Bentley's very high standards. At my GP's insistence, I ended up at yet another physiotherapist, a bustling spitfire of a woman who revealed that one of my feet was collapsed slightly inward, and that I really should be wearing something called an 'orthotic' in my shoe.

'Hang on. What did you say?'

She said it again. Why had nobody ever mentioned this before? Why hadn't I ever noticed it myself? If something had 'collapsed', wouldn't you notice? Rather than fork out $500 for the 'orthotic', I simply popped down to the chemist, spent forty bucks on one of those rubber haddocks you slide into your shoe, and I've had virtually no back problems since. Virtually none. Forty bucks.

Fourteen months after I had last seen him, I called to make an appointment with Dr Bentley. A man's voice answered. 'Is it an emergency, Mr Martin?'

'Kind of. I put my back out by sneezing.'

Forty-five minutes later, I unfolded from a taxi, hobbled past the smokers, the Pissworks and the glass door, and noticed immediately that everything had changed. The reception area seemed larger, brighter – dare I say, funkier. And gone was the girl on the desk. In her place stood Simon, a very fit young man in very tight pants.

'Mr Martin, the nurse will show you through.'

The nurse was a nice bloke who hovered down the corridor and swept me into what had been, when I was last there, Dr Bentley's office. It still was, but the wall dividing it from the next room was gone, and the two halves were separated by a beaded curtain. Clearly visible through the clacking beads was the familiar outline of Dr Bentley, attending to an older woman on a table. And there appeared to be two other patients on nearby tables. They were all receiving treatment simultaneously. He was gliding from one to the other like a TV chef. It was such a bizarre gear change that it took me a full five seconds to notice what was playing on the sound system – 'Smooth Operator' by Sade. The nurse instructed me to take my place on the table. I was halfway there when the beads parted, and there he was, Truman Capote.

It was Dr Bentley, but not as I knew him. He was dressed in a loose-fitting linen suit, and was tanned to the shithouse. The beard was gone, but the 'tache remained. He looked ten years younger. And, yes, he had an earring.

I started to speak, but he quickly gestured me to shoosh. I got face-down for the first time in over a year and he set to work. Head left and right, etc, but no nail gun this time, just a few taps with his fingers, the odd repositioning with a foam wedge, and all the while he's humming along to Sade!

'And you can stand.'

I could barely speak.

'Do you want me to come back next week?' I managed.

'That's up to you,' he smiled. Then, with what may have been a wink, he was off, clattering through the beads to check on his other works-in progress, humming and adjusting without a care in the world. It was quite a transformation. I looked across at his desk. The framed photo of the woman and kid was gone.

Simon tore off my receipt with unnecessary flamboyance and bid me farewell with a Biro clamped between his teeth. I stumbled out into the sunlight, my spine safely back in neutral. I crossed the street to my car. And then I got in. And just sat there for a while.

the notary public

All I needed was fifteen signatures and I would be rid of the whole damn thing. Or rather, I needed the same signature fifteen times. In order to finish the labyrinthine paperwork for a job I thought I'd seen the last of several years earlier, I would have to complete fifteen certificates of authorship, definitive proof that I was the legally recognised author of a particular written work. As the written work in question had not been particularly well received, this was not an authorship I was in any hurry to have recognised so definitively. But lawyers will be lawyers, and so the price of freedom was set at fifteen signatures.

'What the fuck is a notary public?' I enquired of my wife as I emerged from an igloo of paperwork.

'The notary public has to witness your signature fifteen times,' she said, referring to one of three Post-it notes on her wrist.

'That's it? That's all he has to do?'

'That's all.'

'And how much does he charge for this?'

'Five hundred and sixty dollars.'

'Is there a trick to it?'

'What?'

'Is it a trick signature? A special trick signature?'

'It's his normal signature.'

'And there's no other written assessment or memorandum of advice or anything?'

'It's just the signature. We have to go to his house.'

'So, anyone could sign it, really?'

'Not anyone, it has —'

'Hang on, did you say *his house*? We have to go to his house?'

'He's retired.'

'He's retired. And he calls himself the notary public?'

'That's it.'

And there were hundreds of them – retired solicitors, mainly – hibernating in the suburbs, pimping their autographs for seventy bucks a pop. Like elderly pot dealers or voters for the Golden Globes. Bargain-hunters may care to note that if the documents are multiples of same, the price drops to thirty-five dollars per signature, from the second one on. Because then he doesn't even have to read them.

As we rounded the leafiest corner of the leafiest street in town, an expensively ramshackle two-storey house loomed into view. The lair of the notary public.

'There it is,' I said. 'The house that fuck-all built.'

Before we had a chance to knock, the door opened and there stood the notary, looking like a retiree who'd just missed his coach to the Gold Coast.

'I've been watching you,' were his first words, and before we could identify ourselves he'd proffered a limp, translucent hand almost too delicate to shake. 'Nugent,' he announced. 'Did you bring the money?'

My wife held up a cheque for $560.00.

'Correct weight,' declared the signature magnate and, without bothering to ask our names, he ushered us into his place of 'work'.

It felt like every grandparents' house I'd ever been in. A fading commitment to late sixties interior design with a lifetime's accumulation of knick-knacks, duly sandwiched between dust and doilies, and suffused with the smell of bottled fruit and Pine-O-Cleen. Furniture that could have been obtained at auction following the cancellation of *The Don Lane Show*. A bowl containing more wrappers than barley sugars, some keys and a lemon. A large TV remote with a Dymo-tape label pointing out how to switch over to the video. A bottle of port set into a cane stagecoach, a large thermometer set into a ceramic trout, and a leather-bound

Melways always within sensible reach. The dining-room table was covered mostly with junk mail and local free newspapers flattened in preparation for later scrutiny. Some brochures for a retirement village sat defiantly unopened, and a racing form guide was spread across the only cleared space, with enough selections circled to suggest that the signatures had indeed been selling like hot cakes.

'Sit yourselves where you will,' he instructed, clearing away his battle plan for Flemington. As we took the only available seats, he snatched a pen from a pile of many, and ceremoniously removed the lid as though about to compose a requiem for a visiting monarch. Instead of what he was about to do, which was sign his name fifteen times. Realising there was no chair for himself, he scuttled off to secure one from, judging by the result, the early 1970s.

'Now, what's this about?' he inquired, seating himself between us at the head of the Formica table.

'We just need these signed,' said my wife, as had so many before her.

With amusing solemnity, the notary public appeared to weigh the fifteen sheets of A4 in his hands, as if this would somehow tell him more than if he were simply to read them. 'There's fifteen of them, you say?'

'Yes. Fifteen.'

'Then I'll be needing a drink,' he announced, springing to his feet and toddling off to the part of the house where, presumably, that fruit was being bottled.

Under the sound of the notary clattering in the kitchen, I could hear that he had subtly turned on an AM radio tuned to a racing station. 'So, this is the guy? This is the notary?'

'Shhh!' My wife's frenzied hand gestures suggested that, as usual, I was talking too loudly.

'This is the guy, the only guy, who can do what even our own lawyer isn't qualified to do?' I whispered with increasing disbelief. 'And he doesn't even have an office? Where's the sense of ceremony? The notary public's wearing shorts!'

At that moment the shorts and the notary returned, carrying a large jug of what was possibly lemonade, possibly straight vodka; we would never know, because the tray contained only one tall glass.

As the notary poured himself a long cool one, my wife attempted to outline the nature of the documents he was about to endorse with such expensive finesse. But the notary was having none of it and waved her into silence. His mind was elsewhere and may have been there for some time. Details were unimportant. What was important was that we looked like decent enough people and that the name on the cheque was spelt correctly. Halfway through my description of the written work the certificates would authenticate, he blurted, 'There's no GST, you know!'

A series of coughs and retches indicated that the

notary's attempt to retrieve something from the floor under the table was proceeding with difficulty, but after a good minute-and-a-half, he wrenched himself upright and tossed a battered exercise book onto the table, like someone landing a thrashing stingray. Minutes passed as he fumbled for the relevant page, and minutes more as he ruled lines in red Biro and recorded the transaction in tiny spidery handwriting.

I realised too late that I shouldn't try to break the awkward silences by asking the notary questions, as this only immobilised him and prompted answers so detailed and unnecessary I fully expected slides to come out.

'The notary public is a role,' he revealed, 'that goes back to Ancient Rome', as if this would lend weight and dignity to our seedy little exchange. I noted that lots of things went back to Ancient Rome, enforced sodomy for one, but the notary merely chuckled and assured me that there would be 'none of those shenanigans' this afternoon. That, I assumed, would have required a much larger cheque.

Once the financials had been well and truly put to bed, the notary limbered up for what would be a punishing regimen of signatures, one following the other, each one legible, on and on into the wee small seconds of the following minute. He shuffled the documents as though he were about to throw to the weather and, for the first time, actually looked at one – more for targeting purposes than for comprehension or authentication. He could have been signing his own death warrant fifteen times, for all he knew.

And then, bang, he was off. The notary's mighty John Hancock had its way with certificate after certificate of fuck-knows-what until, fifteen well-subsidised exertions later, he collapsed, spent, a notary profligate awash in his own signatory largesse.

In fact, he simply set the pen down and smiled like a child who'd correctly spelt the word 'potato', and that, I assumed, was that. But it wasn't.

'We'll need to add the official seal,' he said, suddenly remembering there was a second part to the ancient charge with which he had been tasked. With an enervated flourish, he whipped a yellowing sheet of mosquito netting off a large object in the centre of the table, revealing what looked like an over-sized cast-iron garlic press standing on the inevitable doily. 'There she is,' he said.

'Does she have a name?' I asked.

The notary just looked at me, as though the concept were somehow distasteful.

'The kids like this bit,' he said, implying that a visit to the notary public was something you might arrange if the new Harry Potter movie were sold out. Each of the fifteen certificates would need what in Ancient Rome would have been a maroon blob of hot wax, glistening in readiness for the notary's brand, but had become in the early 21st century a serrated burgundy sticker, peeled from a roll of Quik Stik 'ancient seal'-style Handi-Labels. His uncomfortably extended attempt to affix the labels was like watching a large baby trapped in some flypaper, and when the phone rang – yes, actually rang – I think he was relieved by my offer to take over.

As the notary attended to the call, my wife took the opportunity to relax the forced smile she had impressively maintained for nearly thirty-five minutes, much of which had been spent on a one-sided discussion of the travails of the notary's football club. 'They need to sack the coach they hired to replace the coach they just sacked.'

I nodded and assumed he knew what he was talking about, because I sure didn't. I simply agreed with everything he said for ten minutes, interrupting only to contribute my one football-related fact. I had read that all AFL players, in addition to their regular training schedules, were being forced to attend week-long classes in what was described as 'the art of footytainment'. This course would prepare them for their inevitable appearances on the many TV shows with the word 'footy' in the title. There was the one where the panel of awkwardly suited boofheads bellowed at one another and occasionally dressed as women. Women being people who were, according to one of the show's keenest intellects, not to be trusted. And there was that other, somehow weirdly gay-seeming one, where the more softly spoken players could be seen sinking into an enormous leather couch, their shoulders draped in pastel-coloured jumpers, as they politely debated the merits of, say, 'the new shorts'.

The notary, while finding my views 'perverse', did agree that the rise of footytainment was a development the game's originators could never have foreseen. 'It's all bullshit, anyway, if you'll pardon my French,' he said, quickly adding, 'sorry, you probably think that's sexist, do you?'

Before I could work out how 'Pardon my French' was sexist, that phone rang and the notary departed, a stray official seal still clinging to his beige cardiganed elbow.

It was only as I sat there, quietly doing the notary's job for him, that I saw it, hanging from the wall behind my wife's head. Some sort of antique firearm. One of those old rifles that appear to have a trumpet for a barrel. The word, I think, is blunderbuss. With our host ensconced in what sounded like a lightly heated discourse with a bookie, I decided to take a closer look.

'Don't touch anything!' said my wife, with good reason.

The gun was a magnificently restored relic, polished, silver and covered in detailed engravings.

'Don't take that off the wall!'

It was a Sergio Leone moment. I had to take the gun off the wall.

'Why are you doing that?'

It couldn't be loaded. It was one of those guns where the user would produce a cloth scrotum full of buckshot, which would be funnelled down the trumpet and packed into place with a plunger. After discharging the weapon, it would be necessary to scour out the barrel with a long bottlebrush. It could take hours to shoot someone.

'You're holding it. Why are you holding it?'

She was right. It made no sense. And, of course, that's when the notary came back in.

The obvious thing to have done would have been to turn to him and say, 'I was just admiring your fine blunderbuss,' possibly lightening the moment with a follow-up line: 'I think we have this exact same one hanging in the back window of the ute.'

Instead, to the horror of my wife, I swung the blunderbuss down in line with my right leg and manoeuvred my way back to the table without the notary seeing what I had done. I have no idea why. Did I feel guilty in that instant; did the very act of holding a gun turn me into a fugitive from common sense?

'Now, where were we?' he said, settling back into his seat and reshuffling the certificates. The gun was resting on my lap. If the notary had looked to his right he would have seen an unmistakably blunderbuss-shaped silhouette, set into the dust on the wall.

It was time for the garlic press to be deployed. He inserted the first certificate and lowered the press with what was surely nowhere enough force to leave an imprint on the seal. But no, this was the notary in his element, and the result was a perfect specimen, suitable for framing. My wife, seizing any opportunity to buy time, spent a full minute examining the seal and complimenting the beaming notary, while simultaneously kicking me under the table. But what was I supposed to do? As the notary set to work on the remaining fourteen certificates, I thought maybe I could lay the blunderbuss on the floor under the table. By the time he found it, we would be long gone and . . . and what? Would he call the police? Why would he do that? He'd just hang it back up and return to his equine calculations . . . wouldn't he?

'Do you people read that bloke in the paper?' asked the notary, now right in the swing of things, working the press with musical precision.

'What bloke? Not . . .?'

But yes, he was referring to the city's most conservative columnist, a man whose vituperative outpourings appeared with frightening regularity in a local newspaper. A newspaper which also frequently reported the latest 'evictions' from TV's *Big Brother* as though they were important news items.

'He's the only bloke who tells it like it is. Don't you reckon?'

At this point I was ready to reckon anything the

notary wanted, just to get out of there. But there was no need. His questions were all rhetorical.

'He's the first bloke who's been brave enough to say what everyone's thinking since B.A. bloody Santamaria.'

B.A. bloody Santamaria was a man who used to say things that these days would be considered appalling by some and 'fair and balanced' by others. For a brief moment, I considered what might have happened had the blunderbuss been loaded, but my sanity returned when I realised how long it would take to reload if I missed. Instead, I panicked and went the other way. 'Isn't that the truth?' I said in a suspiciously high register. 'Where's B.A. when you need him?'

In fact, B.A. had long since passed on, but it turned out that he and the notary had been acquaintances. And this prompted a long story about how they had been watching the football together one day when, in the actual words of our host: 'We both fell asleep and . . . well, that was how that story ended.'

My rapt attention during this stillborn anecdote was, I discovered later, precisely the diversion my wife needed covertly to dial the notary's home number, which she had stored in her mobile phone. Brilliant. The notary excused himself again and as he rounded the corner, I leapt up, charged towards the wall, and noisily reattached the blunderbuss.

My wife said nothing. She'd seen this sort of thing before.

★

As the notary escorted us to the door, I realised that the blunderbuss affair had left me inexplicably shaken. After all, what had I really done – apart from inadvertently holding a stolen gun to the knees of a public official?

'Thank you very much, Mr Nugent,' I said. 'It's been . . .'

'Fascinating,' he said, suddenly flashing a broad grin he could no longer keep under wraps. 'It's been absolutely bloody fascinating.'

Then, shaking his head in quiet amusement, he closed the door. And it was at that moment I realised that the notary was onto us. It would be him who would be dining out on us. For weeks.

As we walked back to the car in silence, a sputtering motorbike pulled into the notary's driveway and a large red-and-black-leather-clad courier cheerfully dismounted and trotted past us. He was carrying a large Postpak containing what I assumed would be, for the recipient, another lucrative distraction from that day's *Best Bets*.

I pictured the courier removing his helmet, handing over the package, and then presenting the notary with a clipboard to sign. A week later that courier would receive an invoice – for seventy dollars.

any old iron

The doctor was staring at my lab report like it was a perplexing weekend invitation from a Mr Alucard of Transylvania.

And in a way, it was.

'Hae-mo-chro-ma-to-sis.' He repeated it slowly, giving every muscle in his face a comprehensive workout.

'But what *is* it, exactly?' I stammered, both in fear of the word and not yet confident enough to attempt it myself.

'Too much iron in your blood.'

Too *much* iron? But all we ever hear is how we're not getting enough. 'Isn't that *good*? Isn't iron supposed to be our *friend*?'

'Yes, but too much of it can kill you.'

'So how much have I got? Like, compared to a

normal person?'

'A *normal* person?' he chuckled. 'Well, your ferritin level – that's the amount of iron stored in your blood – that should be between twenty-five and 250.'

'*Should* be?'

'But for someone with haemochromatosis, that figure can be as high as four or 500.'

'And what's mine?'

He slid the report across the desk and stabbed at the figure with his ballpoint.

'Sixteen forty? I'm *1640*? How is that *possible*?'

'It is very high. In fact, it's the highest I've seen.'

'The highest you've *seen*?'

'I have *heard* of higher.'

I squinted at the figure, but no, the '1' wasn't an ant that had become trapped in the printer. 'Maybe it's meant to be 164?'

'It's definitely 1640. I called them.'

'Sixteen forty must be the time they did the test,' I suggested. 'I feel *fine*.'

'It's no mistake. But it's completely treatable. You're very lucky we discovered it. A few more years and . . .' He let the sentence drive itself to the morgue. Suddenly the weight of all that iron took hold and I felt myself sinking into the furniture. How could this have happened?

'It's genetic. Your parents have given it to you.'

Oh, the irony.

Oh, the iron.

Venesection 1: November 24

Irony 1: I never gave blood.

There are eight fat syringes sitting on the tray. Each one could be used to ice a large cake, one large enough to fit the words 'Welcome Home Haemochromatosis Sufferer' and still leave plenty of icing for the kids. In twenty minutes each of these syringes will be filled with my toxic, rusting blood and, after a tall glass of Lucozade and a short lie-down, I will be taxied home to begin growing a replacement pint with less iron in it. This process is called a 'venesection' and I'll be having one of these, thank you, bartender, every week for the next eight. That's how long it will take me to replace my own blood completely. To reduce my iron levels to normal. To become a normal person.

'So, do you give blood, Mr Martin?' The nurse wedges a pillow under my right arm and starts shopping for a vein.

'No, I don't.'

'What, never?'

'No, I just . . .' Couldn't be bothered. Don't like needles. That old thing about it being 'a whole armful'.

'. . . haven't had time.'

The nurse cocks her head at an angle that says all that needs to be said. All of her tools are individually wrapped in plastic, like an airline breakfast. She tears one open with her teeth. 'Now, this won't hurt a bit.'

But, of course, it does. She punctures my forearm with a small, sharp pipe, plugs in the first syringe and slowly, surely, withdraws the plunger. I feel nothing, but the barrel is a gradually expanding bar of red. It sure *looks* like normal blood from where I'm sitting. I want to ask her what they'll do with it afterwards, but my jaw is clenched tight and I'm gripping the armrest like we're on a rollercoaster, slowly ratcheting skywards.

'Try to relax. Think about something pleasant.'

'Like what?'

'Can't you think of something?'

'Not while you're doing that, I can't.'

'Look, there's the first one done.' She uncouples my inaugural crimson tube and places it carefully on the tray, next to the seven empties.

'It seems like an awful lot. Are you sure it's not supposed to be eight syringes over eight weeks?'

'No, just relax. We've got to get you cleaned out. This is saving your life, you know.'

I know, I know. There are three of us having our lives saved this afternoon, one pint at a time. Three white men, getting whiter.

Venesection 2: December 1

Irony 2: It's the world's most common genetic disorder, yet no-one's heard of it.

This week there are six of us 'Heems' in the room, including two first-timers. I contemplate inquiring as to their ferritin levels, seeing if anyone can top 1640. But no-one makes eye-contact. It's not polite to stare while someone's being drained.

My doctor had suggested I visit the Haemochromatosis Society website, so I logged on, hoping to find pictures of nude women with extraordinarily high iron levels. Haemoerotica. Instead I learnt that approximately one in 250 people in this part of the world suffer from 'iron overload' and most of them don't even know they have it. In some countries that figure is 'as low as one in 300'. As *low* as one in 300? It's a fucking epidemic that nobody knows about!

This week's nurse bites open the plastic packet and strikes at my forearm like a cobra. I try not to flinch, so the newbies will think I'm an old hand at this.

'We're seeing a lot more of you Heems lately,' she says.

'No-one I know seems to have heard of it.'

'Have you heard of cystic fibrosis?'

'Yeah, sure.'

'Well, that's probably the most well-known genetic disorder and that's only one in 2500.'

'One in 2500?' I splutter. 'That's pisswoak! This is literally ten times more common.'

'Well, that's true, but I wouldn't make light of cystic —'

'They've got a shop!'

'I beg your pardon?'

'In Collingwood. I've seen it. The Cystic Fibrosis Thrift Shop.'

'Oh, yes. I think that's closed now.'
'I'll bet it is. Too hard to say.'
'What's your point here?'
'Where's *our* shop? We should have a shop.'

She looks at me like I'm insane. Then she turns to the syringes. Still six to go. She sighs.

Venesection 3: December 8

Irony 3: For hundreds of years, teetotallers have been dying of cirrhosis of the liver.

The liver, that's where it strikes hardest. Your liver fills with iron, and then you die. This can take years, so most people don't start to feel any symptoms 'til well into their thirties. This is why haemochromatosis doesn't have a shop.

It's been gathering speed for sixty or seventy generations, but because it was only spotted in the mid-1800s, and because it was only identified as an inherited disorder in the mid-1960s, and because the test to confirm that you actually have it was only perfected in the mid-1990s, and because nobody can say it, and because we don't have a shop, people are dropping dead all over from cirrhosis of the liver. Non-drinkers, many of them. Non-drinkers who may as well have got fully tanked every night of their abruptly discontinued lives.

But here's the good news. If you get onto it early enough, and have the initial series of venesections, and then have as few as four per year for the rest of your life . . . *you will be completely cured*! And that, my friends, is what makes haemochromatosis the most popular genetic disorder in the world today, the number-one choice of mutants everywhere.

Of course, 'cured' isn't the word. Your genes remain your genes, non-transferable. But the end result is the same. Death can be cheated.

Haemochromatosis,
Haemochromatosis,
Even though the sound of it is something quite atrocious . . .

'But you must remember to keep having the removals, Tony.'

'I know, I know. Look, I'm having one now.'

'Don't make me take you upstairs.'

Professor Helvellin is the hospital's Head of Iron Studies and the suavest damn haemotologist I've ever met. 'Taking you upstairs' is his way of illustrating the seriousness of the condition.

'I have five men in their early fifties.'

'I know you do.'

'By the end of the year they will all be dead from liver cancer.'

'I know.'

'If *they* had been diagnosed in their mid-thirties, they would all be fine.'

'I know that.'

'Do you realise how lucky you are?'
'Yes, I do.'
'Do I have to take you upstairs?'
'No, you don't.'

I have nothing against meeting the five doomed men in their early fifties, but it feels a little distasteful to me, parading my apparent good fortune before them.

'Good. Because I don't really want to go back up there this afternoon. Where did you get that ice-cream?'

'The trolley just came round.'

'Which way did it go?'

'Oncology.'

He exits, briskly.

The nurse and I return to the *New Weekly*. It's the 'Stars Without Make-Up' issue and we laugh and laugh as she extracts syringe after syringe of my poisonous blood.

Venesection 4: December 20

Irony 4: A process designed to save my life nearly killed me.

The blood is draining from the nurse's face faster than she can syringe it from my arm. I'm describing what happened on the evening of my last venesection. The reason I'm five days late.

'I thought I was fine. I thought I was getting used to it.'

'But you should never *run* three hours after a removal!'

'This I now know.'

'The professor wouldn't be impressed by this, Tony.'

'I know. He'd take me upstairs. Really slowly.'

Immediately after your venesection, it is advisable to take it slowly and drink many, many liquids. Not run up the street full-pelt and knock yourself unconscious. But I'd already ordered the burger before I locked my keys in the car, so I had to run up the street, many, many blocks, to get there in time. I hate a cold burger.

I came to on the footpath, the side of my head scraped and throbbing, my hips twisted and numb, both hands hot and grazed, and my glasses unbroken but bent in a knot. How long had I been lying there? In a movie when someone blacks out, there's always someone else around to offer some smelling salts, but the quiet street was completely deserted. There are whole two-, three-minute blocks of time outside your house when nothing happens. When no car goes past, when no neighbour ventures out to the letterbox, when no-one is looking. I had collapsed during one of those blocks of time. If an idiot falls in the street and no-one is there to see him fall, has he really fallen? Discuss.

'Right, you're going to sit there for a full half-hour, Mr Martin, and drink your Lucozade.' She trundles the trolley over to the sideboard and starts loading my blood into something I assume will be consigned to the earth's core.

As I roll down my sleeve I notice another tray containing eight fat syringes, racked up and ready to go. A large man with a pre-rolled sleeve charges in and clambers aboard my vacated chair. He sets up his own pillow and gestures impatiently to the nurse.

'I need to be outta here in fifteen,' he insists.

'Sure,' says the nurse, looking straight at me. 'Knock yourself out.'

Venesection 5: December 29

Irony 5: I'd been taking iron tablets.

The ward is packed and the blood is flowing. It's the post-Christmas clearance.

This week's nurse wants to know how I discovered I had the disorder. It's always a disorder, never a disease, because you can't catch it, I guess. Keep in mind the author's medical qualifications are limited to having Google bookmarked. 'It started with an ear infection,' I say, like Casey Kasem announcing the title of a new Leo Sayer tune. 'I had this ear infection. It went away. Weeks later, I started feeling dizzy all the time. From the moment I woke up I felt like I was on board a ship during a heavy storm. I could barely walk straight.'

'That'd be the ear infection.'

'As I later discovered. But at the time, I'm telling this to my old girlfriend, and she goes, "Don't you have low blood pressure?" and I say, "That's right", marvelling at her ability to remember every bad thing about me. And then she says, "This happened to me. You need to be taking iron tablets." Can you believe that?'

'Was she trying to *kill* you?'

That's what everyone always says.

'But get this. I happen to have a cholesterol thing going on, so I'm getting blood tests done four times a year. About this time, one of these comes up. I'm collecting the form from my doctor, and as I'm leaving – almost as an afterthought – I happen to mention I've been taking iron tablets for a month. "Why would you do that?" he says, so I tell him about the dizziness, and he goes, "But didn't you recently have an ear infection?" I look at him like a prize dick, and he says, "*We might just get them to check your iron levels while they're there.*"'

'So, if you hadn't made a whole lot of uninformed, stupid medical assumptions off your own bat, this never would have been detected. Is that what you're saying?'

Finally, my uninformed stupidity is starting to pay off.

Venesection 6: January 6

Irony 6: I took the iron tablets in Scotland.

Scotland, Ireland, up round there – that's where the trouble started. Sixty or seventy generations back, so the brochure goes, your Celtic type was supposedly so short of iron in his diet, he developed the miraculous ability to retain what little he did have, rather than pissing it away like the normal person. And so he began hoarding it in his bloodstream. Joke-writers will be delighted to learn that for many a Scotsman, miserliness occurs at a genetic level.

But hang on a second, why were they so short of iron? Was there no meat? No green vegetables? No offal? Or was the local food so fucking horrible that the Celts preferred genetic mutation as a means of gaining nourishment? This whole 'one in 250 people' haemochromatastrophe seems to have come about because one Celtic bloke wouldn't eat his greens.

'I tell you, if we ever catch up with *that* bloke,' I say, having just subjected another nurse to the iron tablets story.

'Was your ex-girlfriend trying to *kill* you?' she says.

'I called her up and told her. I said, "You nearly killed me, and then you saved my life." '

'What did she say to that?'

'She started crying. About the second part, I think.'

By complete chance, the four weeks I was knocking back the iron tablets were spent in Scotland, where I was undertaking a speaking engagement. I was dizzy the whole time. So were the people I was addressing, but that was due to having ingested large quantities of piping hot local beer.

What an affront to those ancient Celts. Standing

on their sacred land and filling my face with iron tablets. If they'd had iron tablets in their day, none of this would have happened.

Venesection 7: January 12

Irony 7: I've always made fun of Vikings.

Because haemochromatosis is also rife in Nordic lands, another theory has it that the Vikings brought it with them during one of their infamous 'rape, pillage and, if possible, genetically contaminate' North Sea stopovers. The Vikings were the Status Quo of their day, touring endlessly and leaving a trail of dangerous infections in their wake. They, too, seem to have suffered from a lack of iron. It all went into their hats.

'Do you find Vikings funny?' I ask the nurse.

She doesn't reply. The staff here are getting used to my inane iron digressions. But today, nothing can dull my mood. After this venesection, it's one more to go. I feel like busting out, going on a rampage. I guess it's the Viking in me.

'Har-harr', I growl, aware too late that it sounds more pirate.

She doesn't look up.

Venesection 8: January 19

Irony 8: I'm the healthiest one here.

It is highly misleading of me to suggest that somewhere in Melbourne there is a hospital ward where, at any one time, there are only three or four patients receiving treatment. What an absurd fantasy. All these venesections have been performed in the hospital's oncology day centre. Most of the patients here have cancer. They outnumber us Heems five to one. At first I thought this was clever psychology on the professor's part. Eight syringes of blood is a walk in the park compared with what these people are going through.

The man sitting next to me has no hair on his body and his complexion is deeply mauve. He could be twenty, could be fifty. He is engrossed in the tennis and seemingly oblivious to the network of tubes and wires that sprout from his arms, connecting him to a motley stack of amps, monitors and plasma bags.

The match over, the screen explodes in salute to a merchant whose mental instability has led directly to low, low prices. The mauve gentleman turns his attention to me.

'So, what's this all about?'

'Iron. Too much iron.'

'Christ. There's a lot of bloody things that can go wrong, aren't there?'

'This is a new one. Genetic.'

'Oh, you don't want muck about with genetics. What about that genetically modified. food? That stuff's fuckin' *terrifying*. Giant bloody potatoes! That's some scary shit, if you ask me.'

This man is staring death in the face, but what

really frightens him is a giant potato.

'So, how many more of these do you have to do?'

I can't bring myself to tell him that this is the last one. For the past three weeks I've felt like shit, barely able to crawl out of bed in the morning, but, as with meeting the five blokes upstairs, it's like I feel guilty for not being sick *enough*. 'Not sure,' I lie. 'Could be dozens more. It never ends.'

Oh, the irony.

Professor Helvellin breaks it to me gently. 'The venesections haven't worked.'

'What?'

'Your levels are still dangerously high. We're going to have to give you eight more . . .'

'*Eight more?*'

'. . . starting in a week.'

I am impervious to iron removal.

I am unstoppable.

I am Magneto.

Venesection 9: February 8

Irony 9: If he actually existed, supervillain Magneto would be of enormous help to mankind.

Already one of my friends has taken to calling me Magneto. And I've been asked several times about my 'enormous personal magnetism'. I don't have the energy to do anything but play along. 'Oh, yes I'm very magnetic. Every time I walk past the fridge, all you can hear is pizza menus fluttering to the ground.'

There's a pretty good scene in the second *X-Men* movie where the evil Magneto escapes from his 'plastic prison' by drawing all the iron out of a guard's body and turning it into bullets. At every screening, one in 250 people cheer.

'Haemochromatosis? Dr Magneto will be with you in a moment.'

But there's none of that here. Just eight fat syringes sitting on a tray.

'Back for more, Mr Martin?'

'Just the usual, thanks.'

Venesection 10: February 15

Irony 10: The joke about 'setting off the metal detectors' is actually true.

'Hey, do you set off the metal detectors at airports?' The mauve gentleman hacks out a laugh in perfect time with the beeps of his machine.

'Everyone says that, but I read in the paper that if your levels are high enough, that actually can happen.'

He stares at me. I realise with a jolt how rude my 'Everyone says that' must have sounded. My face turns bright pink and I realise that this, too, could be interpreted as a slight. I return to my magazine.

'Is that supposed to be Anna Nicole Smith?'

'I think that's what she looks like this week.'

As the nurse barrels through the syringes, I provide my customary show 'n' tell from the well-thumbed women's mags.

'What some people will do to themselves,' she says, in both disgust and amusement.

The parade of grotesquerie in the 'Plastic Surgery of the Stars Gone Wrong' issue of the *New Weekly* is as disturbing as anything I've seen in the oncology day centre. While we're all sitting here having toxins pumped from our bodies, we are kept supplied with magazines about Hollywood fucknuckles who are voluntarily having botulism syringed into theirs.

'*That's* Dannii Minogue?' she gasps, putting number seven on tap.

'According to the caption.'

'God, I thought it was Kylie.'

'It will be soon.'

A very pale and completely bald middle-aged woman suddenly erupts into laughter. 'Look at Donald Trump's hair!' she shrieks. 'Page sixteen.'

The room is a storm of paper rustles, as we all race for the page.

Venesection 11: February 22

Irony 11: I still haven't seen *The Iron Giant*.

And, of course, when *The Iron Giant* came out, the floodgates were open. 'Look, Tony, they've made a film about you!'

I stared at the poster thinking, 'His liver must be

fucked.' But it did seem like a good vehicle to publicise the condition. 'How about this for an idea – *The Iron Giant*. A young boy befriends a really fat bloke with haemochromatosis.'

I never had that nurse again.

Venesection 12: February 29

Irony 12: Lack of iron is the world's most common nutritional disorder.

As I had demonstrated, one of the reasons nobody ever thinks they might have too much iron is that we're constantly told we should be wolfing down more.

'Eat more beef, you pathetic worms!' the adverts implore. 'Get some of *this* into you!' they scream, as someone hoves into most of a cow. 'YOU NEED MORE IRON!'

Today's nurse reveals that she herself suffers from a shortage of the heavy stuff.

'Well, if you want any, er . . .' I nod towards the eight brim-full syringes. 'Keep a couple for yourself.'

Later, this exchange prompts a revelation.

Venesection 13: March 7

Irony 13: I really do have what every woman wants.

'Women. Do they *ever* stop going on about their lack of iron? Those ads, those endless black-and-white ads, with that exhausted procession of housewives, pleading desperately for iron. I've got what you're looking for, ladies. I've got what you need, what your body *hungers* for. C'mon, let's get *smelting*!'

I never had that nurse again.

Venesection 14: March 14

Irony 14: If the blood banks accepted haemochromatosis blood from our hospitals, all of their problems would be over.

'So, what exactly are you doing with all this blood?' It's taken me fourteen weeks to ask.

'Some of it is used for experiments, and the rest . . .'

And the rest gets tipped down the sink, apparently.

'Why don't you give it to the blood bank? They're always whining about how they don't have enough.'

'We're not allowed to pass it onto them.' The nurse is shifting uneasily, but the syringe remains steady.

'But it's not like anyone can *catch* haemochromatosis from it. In fact, I'd have thought it was superior to regular blood, what with all that extra iron. I'd have thought they'd keep it on the top shelf, for special occasions. Like the centenary port. Bust it out when one of those women from the commercials comes in.'

She pauses, mid-withdrawal. 'Mr Martin, I don't

mean to be rude, but there are other things to talk about besides iron-storing disorders.'

It's been said before. 'I know. I'm sorry.'

She lowers her voice. 'You see these oncology patients? They don't sit around talking about cancer all day.'

I've noticed this. Last week, two of them got into a heated argument about whether a certain AFL footballer had been decapitated or not. Fortunately, the dispute dissolved into laughter when one of them kept referring to the player by his nickname, 'Pants'. It's impossible to keep an argument going when the subject is someone called 'Pants'.

'Besides, from what I hear, you've never been to a blood bank, anyway.'

Word sure gets around. 'That's true. But I am making up for lost time.'

'You know, we can't pass this blood on, but you could actually be having these venesections done at the blood bank, if you wanted to.'

'You're trying to get rid of me now?'

'No . . .'

'I'm *that* annoying?'

'I didn't say that.'

For a few blessed moments, nothing is said.

'Mind you, I hear that at the blood bank, you do get a pie.'

'I think it's only barley sugars,' she says, wearily.

'I heard pie. And there's an open bar.'

'Uh-huh.'
'And apparently you can book a fantasy venesec—'
'Karen! Can you take over here?'

Venesection 15: March 27

Irony 15: For years I've been eating high-iron cereal.

The TV in the oncology day centre is subject to majority rule, so it's always set on sports. And the ad breaks during the sports are always a deafening parade of clanging reminders to EAT MORE IRON. The word IRON is always forged in metal by a medieval blacksmith and it clanks like an anvil onto the name of the product, which is usually a cereal endorsed by a man in a kayak. You CLANK need CLANK Iron Man Food! CLANK.

I remember when cereal used to go 'Snap, crackle and pop'.

Although less active in sports than even a decapitated footballer, I have always been a voracious consumer of high-iron 'sports drinks' and cereals that clang from the packet like a rain of spanners. Now I am forced to trawl the other side of the cereal aisle, sifting through the sacks of driveway gravel calling itself 'muesli'. Muesli, a product I had until now avoided, for fear it would turn me into that bloke with the beard and bicycle from *thirtysomething*.

'Aren't you a bit late for this one, Mr Martin?'
It has been nearly a fortnight since my last draining.
'I checked with the professor.'

'Did he . . .?'

'No, he didn't.'

'I think those five men are sick of all the visitors, anyway.'

I explain to the nurse how after the last removal I'd been unable to get out of bed for two days. I've had fourteen of these fucking things in sixteen weeks and I'm starting to feel like the 2000-year-old man. At first it was just a tingling light-headedness that lasted 'til bedtime. Kinda pleasant, to tell the truth. Like after two glasses of wine. Now it's like after fifteen glasses and the giant word IRON from that commercial, melted down to make a heavy metal smoothie. The more iron they extract, the heavier I feel. I'm more exhausted than all those exhausted black-and-white housewives put together.

But in one week's time, it'll all be over. Except for the four per year forever, but they'll be a piece of piss after this lot. And besides, I don't want to retire from the game completely. Got to keep your arm in.

Venesection 16: April 10

Irony 16: I love steak!

I haven't had a steak for four months and, by Christ, I'll be having one tonight. A steak the size of the *Yellow Pages*. To celebrate. This is permitted.

For weeks I've been a slave to the 'Healthy Eating For Individuals With Haemochromatosis' pyramid. It's like most healthy eating pyramids, I guess. All the good stuff is squished right up the top in the pointy bit, while all the stuff you're *supposed* to eat is spread out down the bottom, where the pyramid's really wide. It's fucking horrible down that end of the pyramid. Lentils everywhere.

I've overslept my final venesection by a week, but I don't care. I really want that steak. The nurse and I giggle and cringe our way through the 'Celebrities Caught Getting Out of Cars Revealing Unsightly Cellulite' issue of the *New Weekly*, and my 128th syringe full of defective haemoglobin is toasted with a flute of warm Lucozade.

Goodbye, Ladies.

Goodbye, Mauve Man.

Goodbye, magnet jokes.

Goodbye, trying to find a park within seven blocks of the hospital.

Goodbye, being stabbed in the arm every week.

One week later . . .

'*Ten more?*'

'You *want* to go upstairs?'

Venesection 17: April 27

Irony 17: Finally, I've discovered what I was born to do.

I was born to store iron. It's what I do. And I do it better than anyone else I know.

And because of this, Professor Helvellin says I

need to have ten more venesections over the next ten weeks. My levels are still 'alarmingly high'. I've been downgraded from 'dangerous' to 'alarming'. I blame that steak.

'Ten more should do it,' he says, cheerfully. 'Tell me, have you joined the Haemochromatosis Society yet?'

'Not yet. How does it work? Do they have meetings? Get-togethers?'

'I don't know. But if they all got together, it would fill the MCG.'

And possibly reverse the earth's polarity.

The nurses look like they knew all along I'd be back. My usual armchair is plumped and ready. The eight fat syringes sit waiting to be fed. The fish tank is humming, the magazines have been refreshed, and the usual clientele sit slumped and slowed beneath the weight of their respective procedures. Everyone's sick, and all is well.

'You're not the worst case we've had through here, you know.'

Today's nurse is a haemochromatosis junkie.

'What, someone's cracked 1640?'

'Last week I heard about a man with a ferritin level of just over 3000.'

'*Three thousand*? How's he doing?'

'He dropped dead on the tennis court. Never even knew he had it.'

Just like that. And that could have been me. Except for the part about the tennis court. It's terrible: I should be mourning that poor metallic bastard, but all I'm thinking is, *'We might just get them to check your iron levels while they're there.'*

Venesection 18: May 3

Irony 18: Haemochromatosis was given its unnecessarily long name by one Friedrich Daniel von Recklinghausen.

I keep reading that von Recklinghausen discovered the condition in 1865, but didn't come up with the name until 1889. What, it took *twenty-four years* to come up with 'haemochromatosis'? What *were* they calling it all that time? 'Von Recklinghausen's Syndrome', presumably.

'Hey, Fred, will you hurry up with the name! It's exhausting, saying von Recklinghausen's Syndrome all the time.'

Friedrich Daniel von Recklinghausen's page at whonamedit.com claims that the celebrated German pathologist was 'quite a colourful personality' and even quotes one of his most famous jokes. It is a stinging rebuff to those who question the existence of a German sense of humour. Ladies and gentlemen, I give you the comedy stylings of Friedrich Daniel 'Bloody' von Recklinghausen . . .

'To say that tuberculosis lesions contain Koch's bacillus and that therefore the bacillus is the cause of tuberculosis is like saying that the pyramid-like piles of horse manure which befoul the streets of

Strasbourg are due to the many sparrows which perch upon them.'

The nurse just nods and says, 'That's actually a very good analogy.'

'Pyramid-like piles of horse manure?'

'It probably loses something in translation.'

'Still preferable to the healthy eating pyramid, I'll wager.'

The joke clangs like a Nutri-Grain commercial. I'm no Friedrich Daniel von Recklinghausen.

I silently dedicate my latest pint to von Recklo, and make a note to see if anyone's bothered to register the name friedrichdanielvonrecklinghausen.com.

Venesection 19: May 9

Irony 19: Now I, too, have my 'time of the month'.

It's no fun being a Heem, but try being married to one.

The nurse has spotted my wedding ring and now I'm explaining how easy it is to get married in Las Vegas. 'You don't even have to get a blood test any more. Thank Christ.'

The nurse seems to find the idea of a Las Vegas wedding distasteful and screws up her face, like I've befouled the streets of Strasbourg with a pyramid of poo. 'Is that a *proper* marriage?' she says. 'I mean, did you say the *proper* vows and everything?'

'As I recall, most of the vows were covered by the phrase "Yada yada yada", but yes, it's a proper marriage. We have the complimentary key-ring to prove it.'

'So, how's your wife going with all this?'

'Well, for the last few weeks it's been like she's Anna Nicole Smith and I'm that old guy she married.'

'How disgusting.'

'I don't mean literally. Well, not in my case.'

In fact, my wife is coping remarkably well with her husband's diminished capabilities. And the constant barrage of iron-related facts.

'You realise that women with this are to some extent protected against its deadly effects by the miracle of menstruation. You're conducting your own venesections every month.'

'Did you just say "miracle of menstruation"?' says my wife from the couch. 'You can blow *that* out your arse.'

It's a proper marriage, all right.

Venesection 20: May 15

Irony 20: The man sitting next to me has a head full of metal plates.

'Got this iron thing, have you, mate?'

'Yes,' I reply. 'I'm full of it.'

'Me, too,' he beams, tapping his own head. 'Three plates full.'

'Three? Is that the record?'

''Fraid not,' he says, with apparent disappointment. 'Quincy Jones has got nine.'

That's the kind of bizarre fact you can pick up in the oncology day centre. I picture Quincy waking up one morning to discover his bald head fitted with a helmet made from dozens of fridge magnets. 'You little pests!' he yells, shaking his head wildly, the magnets ricocheting off, and occasionally sticking to, his many Grammys.

As my new friend massages his plates, I realise that I have a rare opportunity to give a little of what I've been getting.

'Hey, do you set off the metal detectors at airports?'

'Oh, yeah!' he snorts. 'Haven't heard *that* one before.'

Venesection 21: May 22

Irony 21: Busselton, Western Australia, a town with one of the highest incidences of haemochromatosis in the world – one in 160! – is also the home of the international Ironman finals.

Everyone in the ward thinks I'm making this up. And, inevitably, now that I have introduced the phrase 'ironman' into the conversation, much humour is being generated by the enormous contrast between my own physique and that of a popular ironman of the day, Mr Trevor Hendy.

A room full of cancer patients taking the piss.

But I think they're onto something. Ironman competition?

'Ooh, look, we're running round the beach in

lollybags, now we're kayaking, now we're doing a *third* thing, because we're just so freaking *iron*! Send them all in *here*, then we'll find out who the real ironman is.'

'Just relax, Mr Martin. Think about something pleasant.'

I picture the results of Trevor Hendy's ferritin test. Pissweak, I'm guessing.

Venesection 22: May 30

Irony 22: I have always found the word 'phlebotomy' amusing.

It's a funny word, 'phlebotomy'. It's fun to say aloud.
Try it.
Phlebotomy.
See?
I've been saying it for years. It's like 'lobotomy', but without the disturbing connotation. At least, I think it is. To be honest, I've never bothered to look it up.

Phlebotomy: 'Blood-letting as a medical procedure'. It's just a high-falutin' way, or rather a high*er*-falutin' way, of saying venesection. Instead of blood-letting, which just sounds gross.

Phlebotomy.

I'd loved to have heard Paul Lynde say it.

'It's gotta be phlebotomy!' I declare, as the nurse prepares to broach a cowering vein. The alleged humour of the moment is undermined somewhat by the ugly bruise on my inner elbow, evidence of twenty-one previous poundings. I have taken to wearing only long-sleeved shirts, for fear people will think I'm on the gear.

'Mr Martin, they've asked me to earmark a separate sample of your blood this week, for an experiment. Would you mind terribly if I took a little bit extra?' She holds up a tiny ninth syringe. The runt of the litter.

'What, am I *made* of iron?'

'You don't have to say yes.'

And have medical science on my conscience? In fact, I have been feeling less tired lately. I think I've turned a corner. I'm recovering faster. What difference will a few more mls make? 'All *right*,' I say, grandly offering a forearm. 'If you *must*. Ya goddamn phlebotamists!'

'That's one too many,' she says.

And it is. But once you get a word like 'phlebotomy' in your head it can take weeks to dislodge it.

Venesection 23: June 5

Irony 23: While receiving a life-saving phlebotomy, George Washington died from massive blood loss.

Washington had nine pints removed in one twenty-four-hour period, in an attempt to cure a sore throat. This is what can happen when you take medical advice from the Internet. The sore throat was so bad that he would have been coughing up blood had it not all been siphoned out by his 'doctors'.

For hundreds of years, phlebotomy was thought to be the cure for everything from the common cold to Jewishness. At the end of the nineteenth century, by which time George Washington had long since been folded up and filed away, phlebotomy was finally declared to be 'quackery'.

'Imagine being the bloke who made that announcement. "I hereby declare phlebotomy to be quackery." You'd be dining out on that one for years.'

'How many more of these have you got to go?' asks the nurse, without looking up.

'Three more after this.'

She sighs and continues. The fish tank hums. The syringes accrue.

Venesection 24: June 13

Irony 24: The cab driver thinks I need to have blood put *into* me.

This week's venesection – I've finally stopped saying the p word – was a debacle. It was performed by a student nurse, the hospital equivalent of the new teller at the bank, where everything takes twice as long because he has to keep calling the manager over to explain how the pen works. But you don't want to say anything because you can remember when you yourself were wearing a paper hat labelled 'trainee'. Not even when a needle breaks and your own blood is spraying horrifically across your shirt and trousers.

'Honestly, I'm fine. I'll just go.'

I'm a red, sticky mess.

'Do you want us to call you a cab?'

But I'm already squelching out the door.

I stumble towards the cab rank looking like Mr Orange. The first driver waves me a no and demonstrates his central locking.

The second one winds down his window and raises his single eyebrow. 'Jesus! Whaddappened to you? Do you need to go to hospital?'

'I've just come from there,' I say. 'Do you know of any pubs near here?'

Venesection 25: June 19

Irony 25: One of the first records in our house was 'Any Old Iron'.

And the B-side was called 'Boiled Bananas and Carrots', which, coincidentally, is pretty much all you're left with when you cut iron from your diet. The artist was the great Peter Sellers, and I spent most of my childhood vainly attempting to mimic his flabbergasting range of silly voices. Only now do I understand what he was trying to tell me.

Any old iron, mate? Any old iron? Any-any-any old iron?

The rest of the lyrics were cockney gobbledygook. Something about 'a load of nippers' and 'your ol' watch chain'. What it might mean to look 'dapper from your napper to your feet' was anyone's guess.

Every week the drive to the hospital takes about forty-five minutes and to counter the boredom, I've been rewriting the lyrics of 'Any Old Iron', making it more relevant to the haemochromatosis sufferer.

I unleash the result of my efforts on the unsuspecting nurse, midway through syringe number four, but she pulls me up, one verse in. 'I'm sorry, Mr Martin, I don't understand. Is this based on an actual song?'

'Yes, it's a . . . it's . . .'

She's twenty-three. Madonna is her classic rock. She has never known the joy of hooking her thumbs beneath her invisible suspenders and dancing Dick Van Dykeishly round the room, spouting appalling faux-cockney rhymes to the amusement of her equally shitfaced companions. 'Napper to your feet'? I must sound like a lunatic.

'Never mind.'

One more to go.

Or perhaps another ten.

Venesection 26: June 26

Irony 26: Our genetic deformity has brought the family closer together.

Every single nurse, including this one, has asked me whether I've contacted my family yet. 'You have to warn them,' she says. 'Whether you like them or not.'

Was that last bit something she says to everybody

or has the hospital detected our bad blood in one of their experiments?

'I will,' I promise her. 'I think I may have a phone number for one of them.'

Hardly anyone in my family gets on. Let's just leave it at that. But our genes have been talking to each other in a big way and, as a result, the Martins and their many disenfranchised affiliates are contributing mightily to New Zealand's iron medal tally. Thanks to my accidental discovery, a few others who prefer to remain, in their own words, 'right the fuck out of it', are venesecting like nobody's business. Syringe after syringe of record-breaking Martin crude. And all because a certain horny ancestor liked 'em genetically deformed.

But we're speaking now, some of us, because of all this. I recently met a sister I never knew I had. She plays the violin and has just the right amount of iron in her blood. She's beautiful.

'I guess this makes you a normal person, Mr Martin.' Professor Helvellin seems happy with my report card. 'Two hundred and three. Well done.'

But I had nothing to do with it. All I've really done is sit in a chair and read magazines for six months.

'I'm going to insist on six more over the next six months, just to be safe.'

But before I can put any of this together, he's

guiding me out into the waiting room. 'I'll see you next month.'

His smile and handshake are genuine but measured. I turn to leave. The waiting room is full to bursting.

Any old iron, any old iron, any-any-any old iron,
You look neat, talk about a treat,
Haemochromatosis from your napper to your feet,
Bad news, bud, you've got blood,
That we're gonna have to keep an eye on,
And I wouldn't give you tuppence for your pancreas,
Old iron, old iron.

Just a week or two ago, me poor old Uncle Joe,
Started feeling symptoms of an iron overload,
Got an iron studies test to see what it would show,
Haemochromatosis, mate, it's all the bloody go,
Ferritin test, didn't look the best,
Doctor had a gander and was fairly unimpressed,
He ran from the laboratory, he said, 'I'm getting out',
And twenty-five geneticists all began to shout . . .

Any old iron, mate, any old iron, any-any-any old iron,
You look great, but you'll debilitate,
'Cos you're absorbing iron at a terrifying rate,
No red meat; you're not allowed to eat,
Any pizza but Hawaiian,
And I'd stay away from offal, 'cos it's mostly made,
From iron, old iron.

LOLLY SCRAMBLE

The problem was identified in 1862,
By a load of German scientists with nothing else to do,
Transferrin' iron complexes encoded in the gene,
Blimey abnormalities we've never, ever seen!
They all knew who they'd have to turn to,
Fred Daniel von Recklinghausen,
He'll know what to do,
Sure enough, Professor V was round there like a shot,
He interpreted their findings, said, 'This is what you've got . . .'

Any old iron, any old iron, not just any old iron,
You look calm, talk about a charm,
As another bloody needle is inserted in your arm,
You look made, with a glass of Lucozade,
And a tourniquet to tie on,
But I wouldn't give you tuppence for your mutant genes,
Old iron, old iron.

donkey shines

'Here, take this; it'll calm you down,' said my wife, handing me the controls of our brand-new Nintendo64. I'd been working sixteen-hour days for three-and-a-half years, and this was her way of getting me to slow down. Putting me behind the wheel of a virtual Nascar.

Six years on, the Nintendo64 is now a dusty relic of an earlier age. Compared with today's video games, it seems as outmoded as the Betamax, the Hula-Hoop, the Charleston and reading. But back in the late 1990s – a now-forgotten time, when the name Demi Moore really meant something – fun had a name, and that name was Mario.

I had quickly exhausted the virtual pleasures of Multi Racing Championship, the game that came with the box. Two weeks in and I was already trying to make it around the entire course backwards. In addition, my wife had very quickly grown tired of my robotic intonations of the game's catchcries 'What are you doing?' and 'That's it, you're in the lead!' every time we drove even the shortest of distances. I had located all the 'cheats', as the young people like to say, and discovered which of the inanimate objects on the course could be nudged around the track by one's bumper, and how far. I'd wasted whole evenings by setting the tyres on my vehicle to ultra-slippery and seeing how many of the other cars, those controlled by the Nintendo itself, I could slam into a wall. And, of course, I'd invited my wife to join me on the second controller and then spent the entire game setting up head-on collisions. Anything rather than suffer the indignity of having her kick my arse.

'What are you doing?' she said, doing the voice.

'Relaxing,' I replied, rear-ending her into a concrete pylon.

Then one day I woke up and realised that Multi Racing Championship and I had nothing more to say to each other. It had been fun while it lasted, but now I was looking for a more substantial relationship. That's when my wife hooked me up with Mario.

My only prior acquaintance with the fellow was from the awful movie where he was portrayed, with his usual restraint, by actor Bob Hoskins. But on his home turf, he was a mere cartoon functionary, waddling about at his operator's behest, spouting the occasional 'eye-talian' bon mot. It was the fiendish complexity of the 120 tasks with which the little chap was charged that formed the basis of our intense five-month affair. Every night I went to sleep with Mario's sprightly theme tune looping in my head. But even I realised I was in too deep when I came out with this line, during one particularly tricky manoeuvre: 'Oh, it isn't *fair* that they expect a plumber to be this good at tobogganing!'

Eventually, after thousands of unsuccessful 'wall-kicks', hundreds of arse-sizzling hours in 'Lethal Lava Land' and weeks and weeks climbing that god-damn 'Tick Tock Clock', I finally got to fuck the princess. I'm sorry, that was a dream. I finally returned the magic stars to their rightful owner or some such bullshit, and that was it for the feisty sanitation engineer and me. Now, surely, I could return to the real world and try to remember what the hell it was I used to do with all my time. That's when my wife came home with GoldenEye.

Nintendo fans will recall that *GoldenEye* was a forgettable James Bond movie but a sensational video game, one that still produces a middle-distance look of lingering affection from even the most hardened of today's 'gamers', as I understand they like to be called. The people who created it have since moved onto more elaborate games, but I'm sure they see GoldenEye as their untoppable first album. Perfect

Dark has its fans, yours truly included, but then, so does The Stone Roses' *Second Coming*.

I roamed the halls of GoldenEye for a solid year-and-a-half, and went through three controllers, grinding each one's joystick to a fine powder. Most would have moved on after six months, but I stayed put, perhaps comforted by the security of the game's twenty bordered and unchanging worlds. I had traversed each one hundreds of times in every possible mode. I had combined and recombined all the various cheats, searching for the alchemy of some new variation, one that hadn't yet been detailed on the Internet by someone who looked exactly like me, but twenty years younger.

'Hey, do you reckon anyone's ever done the Silo using only Proximity Mines?' is possibly the strangest thing I've ever said during intercourse, but I know fellow GoldenEye players will sympathise.

There is a universally accepted sign that you have gone as far as you can go with GoldenEye. It's when you spend a long afternoon making your way through the entire game, with Unlimited Ammo, obliterating every last table, chair, window, light fitting, fuel tank, computer terminal, bookshelf and beaker along the way. A methodically executed rampage of door-to-door destruction, utterly pointless, especially as many of the destroyed objects are programmed to regenerate themselves. That level with all the crates can take hours.

Finally, the addict enters the 'trying to do the

entire game with no guns, just slapping people' stage, and that's usually when there's an intervention. I myself went way beyond that level unchecked, and so hours, days and weeks were lost in the labyrinth, as attempts to graffiti every available surface with obscenities while in Paintball mode were followed by long, lyrical strolls in the Jungle with the sultry Natalya. The N64 Natalya was digitally modelled, with non-copyright-infringing vagueness, on the actress who had played her in the movie. That I had actually interviewed this woman a few years earlier lent a ghoulish dimension to these sojourns, and this was often remarked upon by my increasingly Nintendo-fatigued wife.

'Running around with Natalya again, I see.'

'It doesn't look anything like her.'

'Did I see you trying to look down her shirt in the caves?'

'I was reloading her grenade launcher.'

'I notice that now you only seem to play the missions she's in.'

'What are you insinuating?'

'Nothing.'

'All right. Here, take the gun.'

'What?'

'Shoot her in the head, if that'll make you happy.'

'No! I don't like these shooting games. I liked Mario.'

'I'll bet you did.'

Sometimes when we were out, I'd find my mind drifting back to the virtual mountain plains of GoldenEye's Russia. One night when we were at someone's house for dinner, I discovered that the movie was playing on TV. When we took our seats at the table, I carefully positioned myself with a view of the silent screen, as I wanted to see how closely the game followed the film's storyline.

'Tony? Did you hear what I said?'

'Sorry. I was miles away.'

Several thousand miles away. Driving a tank. And like everyone who ever got hooked on the game, I'd had that dream, the one where you wake up one day to find yourself trapped within the game itself. How would you go if it was all for real? They could make a movie of that and it would be absolute shit, but I'd be riveted to the screen, calling out, 'No, you don't go down that corridor! There's three more guards if you go that way! Left! There's extra body armour behind that crate!' And the only other person in the cinema would be nodding in silent agreement. And afterwards we'd go to TGI Fridays together and reminisce about how we used to know women.

But how had it come to this? I had always considered video game addiction to be the province of the bong-addled teenager or the St Kilda-based comedian, not the sensible gent in his mid-thirties who likes to read books and conduct actual conversations with people. Nothing like this had ever happened to me. Not since Game Boy nearly a decade earlier.

'*Bli-ding.*' That was the sound the fat brick of plastic made when I switched it on.

We live in an age where the cheapest mobile phone looks way better than any prop from a science fiction film made fifteen years ago, so it's hard to imagine now just how new and fancy the Game Boy seemed back in 1991. Suddenly the unique trance of the video game, then only achievable at Timezone or on your telly, could be accessed anywhere. On a train, in a doctor's waiting room, at a funeral – with the volume down. It changed our very lives, just as bootscooting and the Tamagotchi would in the months to come.

Bli-ding.

'What is it?'

'Tetris.'

'How does it work?'

'You have to rotate the blocks so they drop into place, form a line and disappear.'

'Do I get to shoot anything?'

'It's just blocks. Rows and rows of blocks.'

'Can I turn that music off?'

'There's a volume on the side.'

'And this is supposed to . . .?'

'It's a game. Don't start with your questioning.'

'I'm not.'

'You think it's funny. It's annoying.'

I can't actually recall who I had that conversation with, but that's how it would have gone. I would never have thought to buy a Game Boy myself, and when someone kindly offered to fit me up with one, as per usual I put them through the mill.

'But, tell me, why would I want one of these?'

'It's fun. Can't you see that?'

'Is there radiation?'

'Radiation? Are you insane?'

'What if I get hooked?'

'What are you talking about? They're blocks. Descending blocks. It's not heroin.'

'You're right. Tetris. It sounds harmless enough. Put me down for one.'

Within a week of my first *Bli-ding*, I was dreaming Tetris. Blocks. Descending blocks. Slowly, at first. Then faster. And faster. And faster. Several times I recall driving up Punt Road and spontaneously changing lanes to fill in a gap between two cars. I was driving Tetris.

There were other games but I recall none of them. The zombie-like state induced by those relentless plummeting blocks was perfect for, say, a long plane trip or an appendectomy. Having very recently endured the latter and embarking on the former, I packed the Game Boy, Tetris and spare batteries in my handluggage. The flight from Melbourne to Scotland was supposed to be several hours longer than the director's cut of *Dances with Wolves*, and with no drug yet invented that could send me to sleep on a plane, I intended to spend much of the trip in an alcohol- and Tetris-fuelled stupor. However, a lightly frosted flight attendant soon informed me that my 'bleepy box', as he called it in fluent Corky St. Clair, might interfere with the plane's controls. I pictured myself achieving Hi Score just as the engines cut out and we dropped from the sky like a cartoon anvil. Through the screams, I'd be peering through a porthole, whispering, 'Please, God, let us land precisely between those two tall buildings.'

I have no relevant recollections of that year's Edinburgh Festival, save to say that of the forty or so stand-up comics I saw perform, only three didn't have a Game Boy reference in their act. The delights of Scotland and its nutbag festivals have been the subject of extensive rhapsodies elsewhere, so I will spare the reader talk of 'neeps' and 'tatties', but one small incident which occurred at Edinburgh airport may prove germane.

Security at UK airports had been severely upgraded since the Lockerbie explosion, and this added a fresh dusting of brusqueness to the already-curt gatekeepers of Heathrow. As we noodled our way through the security cattle pen, I detected a sneering Blakie up ahead, grilling the tourists. To the Americans he would say, 'How long are you staying?' To the Australians he would say, 'When are you leaving?' I was from New Zealand. I got searched. Or would have, had not a floppy-eared security beagle jumped an old lady, causing needle-points of panic as five duty-free bottles of grog exploded across the lino, each one a sharp, shattering flashback to Lockerbie. In the gin-fumed melee that followed, I was hustled to an exit and officially introduced to what I had always heard described as the 'mothercountry'.

But at Edinburgh airport, things were a tad more relaxed. They love Australasians up there, for all the predictable reasons, ranging from 'I hear you hate the British as much as we do' through to 'What's happening on *Home and Away*?'.

On the way through Customs, an officer whose body was three sizes too big for his uniform dragged me aside and started pulling everything out of my bag. Behind me were a hundred people full of Red Stripe and desperate to get the hell out of there. It was no time for a chat.

'Whort's thuss?' The words were extruded – dare I say, bagpiped – from deep within his jutting beard.

'It's a Game Boy.'

'Yu Ostreeliun?'

'New Zealander.'

'Seem duffrunce, unnutt?'

'Sure. Whatever.'

'Su, whort's a Geem Bouy?'

'It's like a . . . calculator that plays video games.'

'Oh, aye. Shoo'us hoe it war'ks, tharn.'

'What, here?'

'C'marrrrn, meetie. Hughmour me.'

To the discernible displeasure of the queue, I was forced to provide this curious Scotsman with a potted demonstration of Tetris. The device was relatively new on the market, but I found it hard to believe that he'd not come across one before. He may have been merely toying with me. Giving me the wind-up out of sheer airport-induced boredom. But minute after painful minute ticked by as he made me take him through an entire game.

'Su whort harpens uff ye doon't gut unney leens ut orrl?'

'If you don't get any lines at all, the game's over pretty quickly.'

'Du tharrt forruz.'

'We don't have time for me to do that.'

'Ye soond a but nar'vous theer, sir.'

'I'm not. It's just . . . all these people are waiting.'

'N'theel be wheeting a lorrt lorrnger if ye doon't givvuz a Hay Scoore.'

He let me off without a Hi Score, but the encounter put me off Tetris for a while. I didn't reach for it once on the flight home. The spell was broken. The Game Boy was chucked in the bottom drawer, where it remained 'til the batteries leaked and the UN were called in. It was a very brief affair, and nothing like it had ever happened to me. Not since Donkey Kong, nearly a decade earlier.

'I'm not going to give you any money. You'll only squander it on lollies and Space Invaders.'

That was a phrase my mother should have put on a T-shirt in the late 1970s. She hung on to it, too, well into the late 80s, by which time the last Space Invaders machine had been carted away to the dump.

'I see on the news they're giving those students more money. I don't know why. They'll just blow the lot on lollies and Space Invaders.'

The day the first Space Invaders machine appeared at the fish 'n' chip shop in Cameron Road, Hillcrest, was a historic one indeed, although I'm buggered if I can recall the date, or even the year. I was still in short pants – I remember that much – and I remember the line up the street, the likes of which hadn't been seen since the day tits had first appeared in the Sunday paper. The Cameron Road Burgerdrome's battered snapper had certainly never attracted such fervent interest, but I knew from talk in the *Waikato Times* that the queue was for Space Invaders, the latest youth distraction off the boat from up north.

I was killed almost immediately. My first twenty cents got me about twenty seconds worth of Space

Invaders and I never knew what hit me. I didn't yet know about hiding over at the side. There was no template for any of this, no programme on TV to show you what to do. No home version. No Internet. No zines. Just leaning over the shoulders of the Maori kids and taking notes. They seemed to have been to a weekend seminar and could ride a single twenty for ten or fifteen minutes. Before long, getting your initials on the glowing orange scoreboard was the talk of lunchtime. Information-sharing networks were established, supported by workshops in the nearby gully, where strategies were drawn up, using sticks in the dirt. Field trips to fish 'n' chip shops across Hamilton were organised, where the more fancied players could be observed in their natural habitat – there were no video arcades yet, so Space Invaders could only be mastered in the fat-fryer steam bath of the local takeaway.

Then, three months in, just as everyone was starting to lose interest, Asteroids arrived. It was blue and different. Soon after that, the owner of the Burgerdrome pulled the covers off Defender and that was it. There were simply no more twenty-cent pieces left. Then came the arcades, the marathons and the kids on the news who were playing Defender for twenty-four hours straight while their parents cheered them on, perhaps thinking they might one day be able to do this in the Olympics.

I had bailed by then, my spare time now fully occupied with amateur filmmaking, silly voices and onanism. It would take something pretty damn special to get me back into one of those piss-stinking arcades. Not to mention a steady source of coinage, which I didn't then possess, as I was on hiatus from my weekend job manning a fruit-sorting machine at an orchard after one of my fingers had accidentally been sorted.

But I could never resist a spelling mistake. And Donkey Kong was surely that. At least, that's what we all thought back then. 'Donkey' was obviously meant to be 'Monkey', what with 'Kong' in there, and what with the entire story revolving around the antics of a large ape. I now hear tell that the whole thing was intentional and that 'Donkey' was a reference to the stubbornness of the protagonist, a tiny plumber called 'Jumpman', who I now realise was an early version of Mario, the aforementioned Japanese Italian stereotype.

Apparently, in Japan, Italian plumbers have a lot of trouble with giant monkeys who steal their girlfriends and hurl barrels at them. This was the plot of Donkey Kong, or 'Donkey Cock' as my friend Wayne Stapleton called it, to much acclaim. So with junk mail delivery money coming in, I was able to spend weeks of after-school time dodging barrels and scuttling up ladders to avoid the wrath of that furious donkey-stubborn monkey. And I was on the board as TFM – three initials, of course, not being quite enough to write a swear word. For six months I was never out of the Top Ten. One day someone unplugged it at the wall and everything reset to zero. By five o'clock that afternoon I had restored TFM to the top five positions.

And then I realised this was madness. Who gave a fuck about whether TFM could dodge more barrels than SAE or PBK? What the hell was I doing with my life? That was the real question. There were other things going on outside. Someone I knew knew someone who actually had a girlfriend. Music had become interesting again. There was something called beer. And other facts started to emerge – large things can be stolen to humorous effect. Cars can be driven through the countryside at speeds well above those suggested. Certain cigarettes make everything funny. Girls have magic fingers. And here I was chasing a fucking monkey up a ladder. Nothing like this had ever happened to me. Not since Pong, half a decade earlier.

I first saw Pong being played on an American cop show. It was either *Griff* with Lorne Greene, *Bronk* with Jack Palance or *Banacek* with George Peppard. I recall two people sitting in a tenement flat playing ping-pong on their TV. It was an astonishing sight, as though a prop from *Star Trek* had appeared by mistake in an episode of *Mannix*. 'That can't be real,' I remember thinking, as the electronic dot blipped back and forth, in black and white, controlled by some kind of tiny joystick on a cord. The next day

I asked around at school. Everyone was agreed; Pong was made up for the TV show and there was no way we'd soon be able to play ping-pong on our TV sets.

Then we heard that someone had come back from the States and that Pong was real.

'Mum, can we get Pong?'

'Tony, don't use words like "pong" in the kitchen.'

We were all still smarting from that screen they sold in the early seventies, the one you placed in front of your black-and-white TV to make it look like it was colour. This was assuming the shot you were looking at had a strip of blue (sky) across the top third and a strip of green (grass) across the bottom. If it was a close-up of someone, it made them look like a face-painted Uzbekistani football supporter.

My stepfather ran a home appliance store, so when proper colour TV came in, he brought home one of the first colour sets in Thames. Word went round the neighbourhood that he would be switching it on at 5pm, and by 4:59 there must have been fifty people squeezed into our front room, with another twenty out in the garden, standing at the open windows. All were hushed and awestruck by the PYE 26 inch, with mock-teak finish, fresh out of the box.

Dad rubbed his hands together, cued up a glass of Lion Brown, and made an announcement to the effect that it was a brand-new era and we were all welcome to it.

'All right, let's see what the future looks like, kids.'

He clunked the knob and there was a twenty-second wait while the set warmed up. Then suddenly, strikingly, there was Fred Flintstone sliding down the neck of that brontosaurus in full dazzling colour for the very first time. Jaws dropped.

'Goodness,' exclaimed my mother. 'It's so . . . *realistic*.'

Colour television was impressive enough in itself. All the old shows seemed to have received a new coat of paint, and for a few weeks everyone stopped complaining about 'repeats'. But the idea that this magic box could also be used to house an electronic game, one as sophisticated as Pong, seemed too good to be true. Either way, it was academic. Pong was not on sale in New Zealand yet. We'd only just got the Mattel Gripper Ball.

Six months later, someone in Thames finally got their hands on a Pong. My friend Grant Bellbird told me his brother knew someone who'd been to the Cluttons' place for tea, and that their kids, Shane and Ricky, were playing what looked like Pong. The Cluttons lived up the other end of town and went to a different school, so there was no way of weaselling our way into their favour. But there was nothing to stop us pedalling up there, sneaking onto their property, and trying to get a glimpse of Pong through a window.

Which is precisely what we did. There was no way

either Grant or I was ever going to get Pong. It was too expensive, and besides, skateboards, movies, marbles, comics, models, felt pens, yo-yos, new ice-cream flavours and Weet-Bix card albums were our first priorities. Pong was beyond our reach. But we could at least cop a perv at someone else's.

Our reconnaissance the previous night had alerted us to a window at the side of the Cluttons' house, with a mess of bushes clustered beneath it. From what we could see through the ranch-sliders at the front, this window would provide us with a clear view of the TV. All we would have to do was wait until dark, walk confidently up the side path so as not to attract the suspicion of any neighbours, slip into the bushes, and hello, Pong!

'What are you boys doing?'

'Um . . .'

'You looking for Shane?'

'Yeah, is he here?'

'No. What were you doing in those bushes?'

'We were going to surprise him.'

'You were trying to see the game, weren't you?'

'Um . . .'

'You're not the first. Now, piss off before I call the cops.'

But Grant wasn't going to let go that easily.

'Please, Mr Clutton, can we have a go at Pong?'

'No! I'm getting rid of the damn thing. It's taken over our lives.'

That night I lay awake, mulling over Mr Clutton's

words. There had been a genuine sense of desperation in his voice when he'd said, 'It's taken over our lives.' He couldn't just have been referring to the stream of gawkers infiltrating his property. And surely *he* had control of how much time Shane and Ricky spent Pong-hogging the TV. No, I got the feeling that Mr Clutton had been putting in a few hours at the console himself. He sure looked like he could do with some sleep.

What a dick, I thought. He's going to get rid of Pong because he's enjoying it too much? That's one problem I wouldn't mind having.

Then I drifted into a dream where I was trapped in a giant Ker-Plunk.

And somewhere in Japan, a man lay awake thinking, 'What if I were a plumber and a monkey stole my girlfriend?'

in the eye of the lolly scramble

Setting off a shitload of Double Happys in the next-door neighbours' letterbox was perfectly acceptable behaviour on Guy Fawkes Night, 5 November, but this was the middle of December. We were laughing like drains, but we all knew we'd be getting the strap.

In the early 1970s it was still commonplace for children in New Zealand to be punished with a few lashes across the open palm, administered by Dad with a blackened tongue of mottled leather, like something you'd use to sharpen a straight-razor. How the miscreant's hand was not instantly severed at the wrist was a mystery. Instead, a flaming, tangy, thrash-handed afterglow lingered for several hours, while Dad unfailingly insisted that it was he who was hurting the most.

My stepfather always included this declaration in his lengthy preambles, along with the additional demand that we wake up to ourselves, stop selling ourselves short, start taking ourselves seriously and promise ourselves we won't let this happen again. There were so many things for ourselves to consider that my stepbrother, Les, often took the opportunity to make a run for it. At that moment, his dad would become an instant blur, chasing him across the couch and up the curtains, peppering his arse with supplementary wallops and inquiring as to whether the squealing absconder had heard a single word he'd just said.

My stepsister, Susie, and I stood there and copped it, keen for the whole barbaric ritual to be over with or, preferably, declared illegal on the news, mere seconds before he brought the strap down. But that particular bulletin was still ten or fifteen years away. In the meantime, getting the strap was as common as the woman over the back, and she was, according to my mother, very common indeed. 'Mutton dressed up as lamb . . . that's gone off,' she once said, but whether the neighbour in question was actual lamb or a chewy, fetid counterfeit, she was probably undeserving of a detonated letterbox. So here we were again, making Dad hurt himself more than he could ever hurt us for the third time since Christmas, when that flare gun 'accidentally went off' in the garage. Everyone had sold themselves short that day.

'I don't enjoy doing this, you know,' he said, rehearsing his swing, and for the first time I actually believed him. Doling out the strap was standard dad business, like the sex talk and secretly letting go during your first ride without the trainer wheels. It was something that had to be done. But this time he seemed distracted, reluctant to go through with it. It was like he knew there would be consequences when Mum got home. Like there was a row on the horizon and he could already hear the thunder.

It was a row, all right, and the only winner would be the local glazier. The three of us stood where we always did, in the middle of the street, and tried to guess which objects were being smashed and by whom. They never hit each other, but it'd be weeks before you'd dare walk through the loungeroom in bare feet.

The bursts of shattering glass provided the only respite from the continuous screaming. Mrs Skerridge from across the road appeared with her milk bottles and cut us a look that said, 'That time of the month, is it?' The neighbours didn't care. They had trouble of their own. And newly installed Pink Batts to keep it sealed indoors, where it belonged. Ours was the only trouble you could hear down the block, but we were beyond embarrassment. We just stood out in the street so that everyone could see we were safe, so that no-one would call the police, so that we'd get our free weeknight movie so that Mum and Dad would have enough time to clean up the scene of the 'discussion'. By the time we got back from *Bedknobs and Broomsticks,* it'd be fixed grins all round, as though nothing had happened. But there'd always be a couple of panels missing from the sliding glass door and several noticeable gaps in the china cabinet.

It was us they were fighting about.

Every thirty seconds, one of our names would escape from the hailstorm of invective. Tony this, Susie that, Les the other. But what had we done to cause all this? You couldn't get twenty minutes of marital warfare out of one cracker-blasted letterbox. Susie was the eldest and the bravest, so she crept along the side of the house and embedded herself beneath the loungeroom window. As close to Ground Zero as you'd ever want to be.

There was no movie that night, just a long, slow wander from one end of town to the other while Susie presented her findings.

The dispute was all about the three of us, and whether we were being disciplined in equal measures, now that we were apparently a family. My mother had suggested that my stepfather was going easier on his two kids, an allegation she backed up with a fusillade of crockery. Dad's view was that her kid was the spoilt one, and to underline this, he reduced a large glass-blown stork to a spray of crystals.

If anything, I felt the opposite was true, on both counts.

I could tell my stepfather didn't like having to strap the new kid. He had his little routine with his own kids all worked out – the patter, the timing, the force of the blows. It had been working for him for years. Now he was taking on someone new, a ring-in. He wasn't across my punishment history. My file still hadn't been forwarded from Te Kuiti. To me, it felt like he was holding back. It still hurt like a handful of Double Happys, but Les always seemed to come off worse. Attempting to flee didn't help, as his backside could attest, but I noticed that afterwards his hand was generally fatter, redder, more useless than my own, and for longer. If we had school assembly the next day, he'd have to applaud by slapping his thigh like it was Oktoberfest.

As for Mum, I couldn't imagine she was riding the other two like she was riding me. She once threw all my comics – enough to fill a bathtub – into the incinerator. A complete overreaction, in my opinion. It wasn't as if they were *all* stolen. But I still recall her frozen look of horror the first time she saw Dad give me the strap. It was the same stunned expression I saw on his face the first time she gave Les and Susie one of her patented mouthfuls. It was all tried-and-true material, well within parental regulations, but it must have been a shock for them to witness each other's punishment character in full flight for the first time. These were characters they'd kept under wraps during the courting months.

When we got home that night, the miraculous restoration had long been completed. A glass-framed photograph of a yacht was missing from above the fireplace, but so was the forced good cheer that normally rose to greet us. Dad was staring at the TV, but wasn't watching anything. Mum was in the kitchen, chopping a carrot for maximum effect. They both turned to us at the same time. Their faces were blank and exhausted, but their eyes seemed to be saying, 'This is all *your* fault. If only you'd been more . . . related.'

The next day we had to drive to Hamilton to buy Christmas presents for our recently doubled number of relatives. The afterpong of the argument hung heavy in the HiAce, and no-one said a word as we ripped through the countryside. No jokes, no Jelly-Tips, no joy to be had.

All the other brothers and sisters we knew had the same mothers and fathers. This whole 'unequal discipline' thing, or *whatever* it was, wasn't a issue for them. No, we had apparently discovered a whole new way to drive your parents crazy – not doing anything. Just sitting back and letting them fight it out amongst themselves.

I wound down the window to release some of the tension and ran a mental inventory of all my friends' parents. None of them had that look. That crazed look that said, 'I don't actually *know* half these kids, but now I'm responsible for them.' It was around this time *The Brady Bunch* started, and didn't *they* make it look easy? We all hated that show.

On the outskirts of Hamilton, Dad finally broke the silence by declaring his intention to 'pull over for a slash'. He veered off into a rest area and disappeared into a cement block piss-bunker marked Gentlemen. The rest of us sat in the van and listened to The Carpenters. Then I, too, had to go.

Jandals slapping on the concrete floor, I rounded the corner to find him standing at the basin, completely drenched. It was one of those taps. He wheeled round, his glasses dripping, and behind them, his eyes aflame with rage.

'What?' he roared.

'Nothing,' I squeaked in reply, and for a few seconds we both stood there, trying to work out how we'd ever come to be acquainted.

Is it just us? That's the question I'm asking myself as Mum hauls me through the Christmas crowds at the D.I.C. We've split up genetically, with Dad, Susie and Les casing Hallensteins, while Mum and I melt into the swirl at the city's biggest department store.

It couldn't just be us, could it? Look at all these people. They sure look happy. They all look like they've taken two barrels of Christmas cheer full in the face. It's sunburn weather outside, but in here the registers jingle, and the music's Der Bingle. Spend All Ye Faithful. I scan the crowd for a child crying, a misfit or a sullen, distant youth. Someone else not buying into the enforced seasonal joy. But they're all oohing and aahing and trying things on.

Mum cuts me loose in the toy department and heads for what I have no doubt will be the most boring part of the store. Probably that place with all the big bolts of fabric. You can feel yourself getting older while you wait for her to finish up in there.

There's a queue for Santa, but I ain't biting. I woke up to that fat fraud a couple of years back. North Pole, my arse. Let the gullible pre-schoolers line up for his cheap shopworn theatrics. I'll be over here doing something more mature. Like trying to find Lowly Worm in the new Richard Scarry.

I'm bent down, inspecting the ape-hangers on the new Raleigh 20, when I hear it. A man's voice, shrill and ragged, slashing through the tinny canned carols. 'Enough!' it roars. '*Enough*, ya hear me?'

Then there's a sound like hailstones glancing across lino. And some screams. A light bulb explodes. There's whizzing and pinging all around me. Something shoots past my ear and rattles to the floor.

It's a jube.

I clamber briefly to my feet.

Santa's going mental. 'You little *shits!*' he croaks, scooping into his sack of lollies and flinging fistfuls, with venomous intent, into the backs of the scattering kiddies. 'You *fucking little shits!*'

He's a red and white blur, spittle erupting from his beard and splintering grenades of confectionary branding, branding, *branding* the bawling, tumbling toddlers. He swings in my direction and manages three sharp handfuls before a phalanx of angry dads decks him with a tackle and drags him, still shouting obscenities, still piffing lollies, into the grotto for a festive beating.

It all happens in less than fifteen seconds.

But as I lie there, face down in the bike aisle, sweet pellets of anger bouncing off the spokes above me, I feel happier than I've felt in weeks.

acknowledgments

My Nevada bride, Annie Maver, was the earliest supporter of these scribblings. She showed them to editors Jo Higgins and Jill Griffiths, and it was author Andy Griffiths who led me to Cate Paterson at Pan Macmillan. Alex Craig was the one charged with turning it all into some kind of book, and this was achieved with the guidance of editor Sarina Rowell and Te Kuiti's own Anne Reilly. Kudos is due to you all, though I have no doubt that each of you will suggest that, surely, I can come up with a better word than 'kudos'.

For helpful suggestions and much encouragement, I salute my friends Janine Evans, Judith Lucy, Greg Sitch, Gary McCaffrie, Shaun Micallef, Therese Barry, Sue Bignell, Nikki Hamilton and, of course, Melbourne identity Mick Molloy.

Thanks also to Hatem Salem, Christine Woodruff, Anita Jupp and Christine Rau, the author of an excellent article about haemochromatosis which originally appeared in *The Weekend Australian Magazine*. And finally, anyone who attempts to write with humour about the world of amateur dramatics surely does so in the shadow of Michael Green's hilarious and definitive *The Art of Coarse Acting*.

THEME FROM *SKIPPY*
Written by Eric Jupp
Reprinted by kind permission of Anita Jupp.

'THE GAMBLER'
written by Donald Alan Schiltz, Jnr.
Courtesy of Sony/ATV Music Publishing.

'MIDNIGHT BLUE'
written by Lou Gramm/Bruce Turgon
© 1987 Stray Notes Music
For Australia and New Zealand: EMI Music Publishing
Australia Pty Limited International copyright secured. All
rights reserved. Used by permission and Reproduced by
permission of Warner/Chappell Music Australia Pty Ltd.
Unauthorised reproduction is illegal.

'DROP THE PILOT'
Words and music by J. Armatrading
© Giftwend/Universal Music Publishing P/L
Reprinted with permission. All rights reserved.

'CEMETERY POLKA'
written by Tom Waits
Reproduced by permission of Warner/Chappell Music
Australia Pty Ltd. Unauthorised reproduction is illegal.

'MEAN TO ME'
Written by Neil Finn
Mushroom Music Publishing

'ANY OLD IRON'
Original lyrics by C. Collins/E. Shepard/F. Terry
© Herman Darewski Music/MCA/ Universal Music
Publishing P/L
Reprinted with permission. All rights reserved.